BASICS
INTERIOR DESIGN
02

exhibition design

Ethical: aware-
ness/
reflect-
ion/
debate

ava
academia

= AN AVA BOOK

Published by
AVA Publishing SA
Rue des Fontenailles 16
Case Postale
1000 Lausanne 6
Switzerland
T +41 786 005 109
E enquiries@avabooks.com

Distributed by
Thames & Hudson (ex-North America)
181a High Holborn
London WC1V 7QX
United Kingdom
T +44 20 7845 5000
F +44 20 7845 5055
E sales@thameshudson.co.uk
www.thamesandhudson.com

Distributed in the USA and Canada by
Ingram Publisher Services Inc.
1 Ingram Blvd.
La Vergne TN 37086
USA
T +1 866 400 5351
F +1 800 838 1149
E customer.service@ingrampublisherservices.com

English Language Support Office
AVA Publishing (UK) Ltd.
T +44 1903 204 455
E enquiries@avabooks.com

© AVA Publishing SA 2011

ISBN 978-2-940411-38-2

10 9 8 7 6 5 4 3 2 1

Design by
Dechant Grafische Arbeiten, Vienna

Production by
AVA Book Production Pte. Ltd., Singapore
T +65 6334 8173
F +65 6259 9830
E production@avabooks.com.sg

All reasonable attempts have been made to trace, clear and credit
the copyright holders of the images reproduced in this book.
However, if any credits have been inadvertently omitted, the publisher
will endeavour to incorporate amendments in future editions.

= **SEED CATHEDRAL,
EXPO 2010**
Shanghai, China

DESIGNER
= **THOMAS
HEATHERWICK**

DATE
= **2010**

Introduction

The aim of this book is to provide a better understanding of the complexity of exhibition design, by exploring the role of the exhibition designer as a creative practitioner serving a multi-billion dollar global industry.

Symbiotic and experimental in nature, exhibition design overlaps a wide range of design subjects in order to communicate clearly. In terms of spatial intervention, interior design is its closest relative. Exhibition design is often a reflection or, indeed, driver of contemporary fashion and style. It is familiar with interior and furniture scale and is concerned with space, form and surface. However, unlike interior design, exhibitions can, when required, stand independently from architecture and see spatial relationships predominantly in terms of the opportunities they provide for communication and display.

Using imagery, case studies, and practical advice, this book will lead the reader to a better understanding of the skills and methods required for designing the narrative and an ability to apply them to their own work.

Exhibition designers need to be curious about everything, not least the idea of theming, which is often seen as the interpretive 'hook' on which to hang a story. The theatrical opportunities borrowed from multimedia, sound, lighting design and a range of other exhibition technologies, create interesting opportunities for storytelling through performance.

The combination of image and text through large-scale graphic design remains a key method of communication to an increasingly technologically and visually literate audience. The easy wealth of access to vast amounts of information have helped to transform the traditional 'graphic panel' hanging on the wall, to interactive, multi-layered and often multi-sensory touch-screen experiences with the capacity to navigate the visitor through complex layers of information.

One of the most stimulating challenges for the exhibition designer is the exploration and experimentation involved in the search for the most appropriate communication media within engaging interactive environments.

= **EXHIBITION STAND FOR KEMITRON,** Germany

Whether cultural or commercial in nature, it is the idea of communicating a story in space that acts as the link between all forms of exhibition design.

How to get the most out of this book

This book introduces different aspects of
exhibition design, via dedicated chapters
for each topic. Using a variety of examples
from both students and professionals,
the processes and strategies involved in
designing space for exhibition are
examined, analysed and debated.

SECTION HEADERS
Current section headings are clearly named
in the navigation bar. The numbers of topics
within the chapter are indicated by vertical
dividers. Past and future section headings are
displayed above the navigation bar.

SECTION INTRODUCTIONS
Each section is introduced by a
few brief paragraphs.

\ Designing for people \   / Student case study /

Exhibition design Understanding the story

052/053

Whether an exhibition is about
a collection, an idea or a brand,
the exhibition designer needs
to clearly understand what the
client hopes to achieve from the
exhibition. What is its purpose
and how will the messages
communicated by the exhibition
leave its audience changed?

Cultural and commercial messages

In considering exhibition objectives,
let us consider two very different types
of exhibition with similar themes. The
first is about recycling, a temporary
exhibition at a science museum called
'Wash 'n' Squash', and the second is
a commercial exhibition stand at a
public environment show for a company
that sells 'Ewash', a non-toxic, wildlife-
friendly washing power.

Cognitive objectives relate to the
important information we want the
audiences to learn about recycling
and 'Ewash'. Research has suggested
that on average audiences leave an
exhibition with six new pieces of
information. In these two scenarios
how would the six key messages be
effectively communicated?

Emotional objectives address how we
want our audiences to feel as a result of
their visit. Visitors to 'Wash 'n' Squash'
have played with a series of interactives
about recycling supported by family
centred graphics, and so feels positive
and motivated. The evocative wildlife
imagery of the 'Ewash' stand
has made the audience feel good
about a brand that is helping to look
after natural habitats.

Behavioural objectives consider how
visitors may change their behaviour
as a result of their exhibition experience.
Have the exhibitions influenced our
respective audiences to make more of
an effort to recycle or change to using
environmentally friendly cleaning
products? Clearly, if this is the case,
the exhibitions have been successful
in their proposed aims and objectives.

□ **PHILIPPINES PAVILION**
   WORLD EXPO 2008
   Zaragoza, Spain
   DESIGNER
□ **ED CALMA**
   DATE
□ **2008**

The overall theme of Expo 2008 in Zaragoza
was 'Water and Sustainable Development'.
The design of the pavilion aimed to raise
awareness of rising sea levels, which are
of particular concern to the people of the
Philippines. The interior of their pavilion
featured a series of large 'bubbles' carrying
messages. The blue lighting effects added
to the overall 'watery' environment.

: WALLY OLINS
...to be really effective you have to be
able to sense the brand. You may
even be able to touch it and feel it.
So that it manifests the core idea.

PULL QUOTES
Thoughts from well-known designers
and exhibition experts provide insight
into the world of exhibition design.

Exhibition design Exhibition space

044/045

● **THE GREAT HALL,
NATIONAL RAILWAY MUSEUM
York, UK**
The artefacts in York's Railway Museum
are not only historically significant, but
many are awkwardly large and very heavy.
Specialists are required to move these
objects and will need to know from the
designer and curator exactly where they
are to be placed early in a design scheme.

● **AN EMPTY HALL
AT EXCEL
London, UK**
At the start of a
commercial exhibition
project, the 'site' only
exists on plan. At this
point, the actual venue
is an empty void.

What is the context of the new exhibition
within the existing building? The
designer will need to consider how to
design a transition space for visitors
entering and leaving the space. For
larger sites, how will visitor flow be
managed? Are there views to the outside
that may influence the orientation of
the exhibition? What is the journey from
the car park to the exhibition? Where
are the facilities? How will the visitors'
experiences be managed?

Most major cities throughout the world
offer purpose-built exhibition halls that,
in essence, are vast empty voids waiting
to be filled with exhibition paraphernalia.

The exhibitor's manual will provide rules
and regulations about stand heights,
access to services, use of materials
and the ability to hang lighting rigs from
the roof. All this information will inform
the heights required for branding,
sight-lines from entrances, visitors' flow
and access, all of which will, in turn,
influence design decisions and help
maximise the impact of the brand.

Whatever the nature of the exhibition,
a thorough understanding of the site
provides an envelope in which the
design team can work, a context for
consideration and, on occasion,
inspiration.

SIMPLICITY AND FLEXIBILITY
The designer of a travelling international
exhibition has much to consider: different
venues, a range of languages, security,
transport and insurance issues, knowledge
of services, lighting and existing context,
cultural and religious understanding.
Rules on set-up take time and complications.
Simplicity and flexibility are the keys.

Orientation
Wayfinding, informing visitors by way of signposts, maps, and trails,
where they are, and where they are going.

CAPTIONS
Detailed captions give
information on the
specifics of each project
and the thinking behind
the design decisions
taken.

RUNNING GLOSSARY
Key terms are explained
clearly and precisely
within their context.

THINKING POINTS
Key design concepts
and some of the debate
surrounding them.

STUDENT CASE STUDIES
Examples of student work
enable the reader to see how
theory is put into practice.

Designing a narrative Student case study

084/085

PROJECT
● **EXHIBITION STAND FOR
'MINI CONCEPT' AT
FRANKFURT MOTOR SHOW**

DESIGNER
● **MELISSA PEARCE**

DATE
● 2010

The ribbon theme conveys the
excitement of a racing track
while the arches suggest a
sense of control, reflecting the
handling power of the MINI.

For this project, the student chose to
design an exhibition stand for the launch
of two new concept cars in celebration of
MINI's fiftieth birthday: the MINI Coupé
and the MINI Roadster.

At the concept model stage two possible
concepts emerged; one using the idea of
a 'ribbon' of racetrack through the stand,
the other a series of arches evocative of
'matchbox' cars. In the final design, a
combination of these three-dimensional
elements was used. Both initial sketch
ideas were expressed in the final
computer-generated client visuals. The
stand also offers an exclusive giveaway
in the form of an 'Airfix' coupé 'kit',
allowing visitors to build their own scaled
model of the car. This idea is echoed on
the stand at full size, adding a sense of
playfulness to the brand message.

The final design effectively combines the
cheeky MINI spirit and the racing pedigree
of the MINI Coupé.

● A concept model of
the stand.

● A concept model of the
ribbon racetrack element.

● Computer-generated views
showing the final overall design
for the stand.

? Imagine you have been asked to design a single-storey exhibition stand
for a well-known mobile phone company at a major trade show in America.
The space will be a 6 x 8 m (19 x 26ft) peninsular site, open on three sides with
a 5m-high wall along one of the 6 m (20ft) sides. Elements can be hung from
the venue roof, but must not be more than 4m (13ft) high from the ground.

1 Your client requires a welcome area, a small bar and seating area for
hospitality, an area for an interactive display and a more private area with
Internet access for private discussion. How can you effectively design
for the needs of your client in such a small space?

2 Using the idea of 'mobile communication for an international business
market', explore possible spatial ideas through a series of two-dimensional
sketching and three-dimensional modelling. Can you identify the strongest
of your ideas?

3 How will your preferred concept support the client's message?
Where will you apply the company logo to best effect?

4 How will visitors to the stand use the space? Is it possible for some area to
be multi-functional? How will the exhibition 'stand out' from the competition?

QUESTIONS AND EXERCISES
Questions in summary allow the
reader to consider how they might
approach a design project.

Commercial trade fairs, brand experiences, themed attractions, world expositions, museum galleries, visitor centres, historic houses, landscape interpretation and art installation are all areas that can be categorised under the broad umbrella term of 'exhibition'. Exhibitions may be permanent or temporary, with a shelf life of five years or five days. They may vary in scale from small table-top displays to the size of a small city in the case of world expositions.

However, whether commercial or cultural in nature, it is the idea of communicating a story in three-dimensional space that acts as the link between these very different environments.

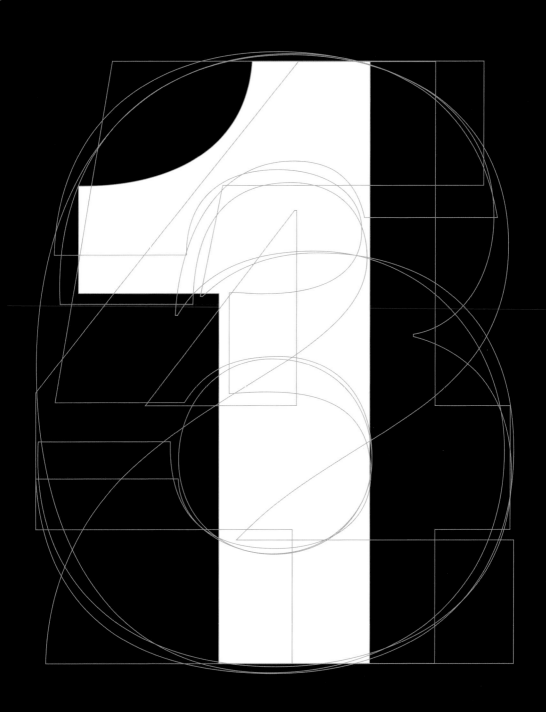

What is an exhibition? Expos

The origins of large-scale exhibitions are French: Paris hosted many of the most memorable expositions between 1848 and 1937. The French word for exhibition, 'exposition', has become synonymous with large-scale events of this type and in 1928 the Bureau International des Expositions or International Exhibitions Bureau (BIE) was set up in Paris. Since then, the BIE has been recognised as the sanctioning body for international expositions. The name 'expo' first came into use by the BIE during the 1960s, as a commonly used shorthand for large public exhibitions on an international scale. Interestingly, expos are now considered the cultural and economic equivalent to the Olympic Games.

World expos fall into two main categories: registered expositions (formally known as universal expositions), and smaller recognised expositions (formally known as international or specialised expositions).

Registered expositions

Registered expositions take place every five years and are on a huge international scale. Since 2000, an increasing number of non-governmental organisations have taken part. They have overarching themes with which participants engage. In Shanghai in 2010 the theme was 'Better City: Better Life', reflecting global concerns about the environment and sustainability. For these grand events, participants are expected to design and build their own pavilions. The contemporary nature of expo encourages experimentation in new media and materials and has traditionally provided the opportunity for innovations in art, architecture and design. However, the high costs of building are often prohibitive for developing countries who may choose to build using cheaper modular structures or, more commonly, share exhibition space with others inside buildings provided by the host nation.

= **THEMATIC PLAZAS AREA
WORLD EXPO 2008**
Zaragoza, Spain

DESIGNER
= **VARIOUS**

DATE
= **2008**

The 2008 exposition in Zaragoza in Spain is an example of a recognised expo. The theme was 'Water and Sustainable Development' and the event was particularly well attended by countries where water is an important national issue. Here we see three themed pavilions: 'Thirst', the mirrored, bubble-like structure inspired by a mountain of salt, 'Beacon', designed to be as efficient as possible in its use of energy, and 'Extreme Water', which took a deep look at environmental disasters such as flooding and tsunamis. Its design was inspired by a wave crashing on the beach.

: PRESIDENT WILLIAM MCKINLEY
Expositions are the time-keepers of progress. The records of the world's advancement. They stimulate the energy, enterprise and intellect of the people, and quicken human genius. They go into the home. They broaden and brighten the lives of the people.

What is an exhibition? Expos

= **ATOMIUM, 1958 WORLD FAIR**
Brussels, Belgium

DESIGNER
= **ANDRÉ WATERKEYN**

DATE
= **1958**

The Atomium, built for the 1958
Brussels Expo, has, like many other
structures built for expo, become a
much-loved iconic symbol for the city.

Recognised expositions

Recognised expositions usually take
place in the years between registered
expos and are smaller in scope.
Recognised exhibitions are usually
linked by more specialised themes
or by national events of particular
significance. Usually the host
committee will build a prefabricated
structure within which participants rent
space. The existing structure acts as
a skeleton on which nations 'hang'
messages about their national identity.

Infrastructure and regeneration

Twenty-first-century expos can attract
over 100 million visitors, requiring vast
expense and many years of planning
by the host country. An extensive
supporting infrastructure of transport
links, accommodation, technology,
health and food is required, and security
issues have also become a key twenty-
first-century concern.

Expos have always been seen as an
opportunity for the regeneration of a city
and experimentation in urban design.
Chicago in 1893, Paris in 1900 and Montreal
in 1967 all built their metro systems to
support world expos and the high speed
magnetic train, 'Maglev', was built to
transport visitors from Pudong airport
to the Shanghai 2010 site. Whilst many
pavilions are seen as temporary structures,
in recent years exposition organisers have
taken the opportunity to design buildings
with a sustainable future to serve their
local and national communities once
the expo is over.

Whilst derelict sites are a sad reminder of
the financial disaster of some expos, others
put the host city on the map; before its expo
in 1988, Brisbane was an insignificant town
on the northeast coast of Australia. Seville
1992, staged in the same year as the
Barcelona Olympics, was seen as a highly
successful branding exercise designed to
finally establish post-Franco Spain on the
world stage as a modern democracy.

All the fun of the fair

Expos are a celebration of human achievement; extending the idea of spectacle to its limits. From George Ferris's great fairground wheel in Chicago in 1893, or the monorail built for Seattle's World Fair in 1962, to the eccentricities of giant butter sculptures and colourful if sometimes incomprehensible parades, visitors to expos expect to be delighted and amazed. The first sewing machine, typewriter, television, telephone, lift and travelator were all seen at expos.

Expos were seen as an opportunity for contemporary artistic and architectural expression. In Paris in 1937, the centrepiece of Spain's Republican Pavilion, designed by Luis Sert, was Pablo Picasso's 'Guernica', now considered by many art historians as the most significant war painting of the twentieth century. In contrast, the Montreal Expo 1967 heralded the birth of IMAX cinema, and continues to take the lead in this particular form of film-making today.

Architecture, in particular, has found freedom for experimental expression at expos. Le Corbusier's Pavillon de L' Esprit Nouveau; in Paris 1925, was considered so shocking that the organisers erected a six-metre-tall (20ft) fence to protect the public. The same exposition saw the launch of the art movement later called art deco, which was to be a dominant international style between the two World Wars. The iconic Barcelona chair, designed by Mies van de Rohe for the German pavilion in Barcelona 1929, was actually intended for the King and Queen of Spain to sit on when they visited the pavilion.

The 1889 Eiffel Tower is the most famous national icon built for an expo, but the Atomium in Brussels in 1958, Seattle's Space Needle in 1962, and the observation towers built for the New York Expo of 1964 all still stand and have become much loved iconic symbols for their cities.

Exhibition

Any organised assemblage of exhibits that is designed to serve an overall purpose or present a theme or narrative.

What is an exhibition? Commercial exhibitions

= **IDEAL HOME EXHIBITION**
London, UK

DATE
= **1957**

Public shows are open to everyone and the UK's 'Ideal Home Exhibition' is a well-known example. Public shows share many of the objectives of trade-only shows, but tend to deal with themes which are of particular interest to the general public. Lifestyle, homes, food, hobbies, home technologies, social, economic and political issues are all examples. Unlike trade-only shows, a different, jargon-free voice is required so that everyone can understand what is on display.

Today, commercial exhibitions are most commonly referred to as trade fairs or consumer shows and, as the name suggests, are concerned with the display and economic promotion of commercial goods and services. Global in scale, virtually all commercial industries engage with a range of trade-show activities servicing not only major companies, but also cascading down through all the subsections of an industry network. Every imaginable product and service, from widgets to aircraft, is presented at commercial exhibitions. Although approximately 90 per cent of exhibitions are trade-only shows that are less visible to the general public, they form a multi-billion dollar industry that helps drive the world's economy.

The role of a trade show

A trade show takes place when businesses or companies of a similar type get together for an event to discuss, sell and network with each other. The shows reflect the current trends in their industries and aim to be forward looking. For many manufacturing companies, this is the closest they come to having a 'shop window' for their products or services.

Trade shows fall into two distinct categories: 'trade only', and 'public shows'. Public shows are usually the largest. The primary aim is to sell, although it is also an opportunity to launch new products, raise brand profiles, establish brand identity or take the opportunity to change how a brand is perceived. Professional bodies representing particular industries often exhibit at trade shows in order to stimulate debate about important industry issues. Most importantly, trade shows are an opportunity for human interaction and all will hope to attract new customers through the use of this sophisticated marketplace for the twenty-first century.

By their very nature, trade-only shows cater predominantly to the business community and the design requirements of an exhibition stand or support facilities will reflect the needs of this specialist audience.

Exhibition organisers

Trade shows are run by exhibition organisers. They create the event, brand and market it, hire the space and sell it on to individual exhibitors. The 'exhibitors' manual' outlines rules and regulations for participants, giving instructions about the availability of electricity, water, lighting, maximum height restrictions and important health and safety information, regarding materials, construction and timescales. Exhibitors are not allowed to obstruct walkways or other public areas and compliance is part of the exhibitor's contractual requirements. These last from registration to the moment a company leaves the venue following a show. Non-compliance with the rules usually brings with it expensive financial penalties and may mean an exhibit is closed down.

: **MAUK DESIGN**
Fill the mind, not the space.

Branding

In the trade-show context, an exhibition stand is a three-dimensional expression of single or multiple brands under the same corporate umbrella. Usually a brand will represent a portfolio of products and will be managed by a brand project manager. A key motivation for the exhibitor, and the challenge for the exhibition designer, is to find ways of successfully marketing the brand via messages communicated not only by the exhibition stand, but also through a range of virtual and paper-based material. This may include a website, interactive material, leaflets, catalogues, film, TV advertisements and merchandising through give-aways. All this material needs to be instantly recognised as belonging to a particular brand image. A logo is a graphically designed symbol that identifies the brand at a glance and is an essential tool for marrying different types of two- and three-dimensional brand materials together, but more importantly connecting the user or customer directly with the brand.

The brand logo could be seen as the visual 'glue' that helps to give a brand a consistent identity. The research and development of a logo is therefore an expensive undertaking and the golden rule for any exhibition designer is to never alter the logo in any way. The exhibition designer needs to recognise that the exhibition stand is a crucial part of the brand manager's marketing strategy. It is a large-scale brand beacon that pulls visitors on to the stand, and acts as a hub for throwing brand messages out into the marketplace. The effective use of graphics through images and text is key. However, text should be kept to a minimum, with more reliance on logos, engaging imagery and straplines. Time pressures and the nature of exhibition culture mean that visitors do not want to stand and read large amounts of text; the designer has a few seconds to get across important messages. All detailed information needs to be provided as digital or hard copy to be accessed at another time.

= **BESPOKE STAND**

DESIGNER
= **PHOTOSOUND**

DATE
= **2010**

Bespoke exhibition stands may be built as a one-off for a particular show, or components of the design might be reconfigured for different international venues. It is this type of stand that poses most challenges for the professional exhibition designer and their design approach will be considered later in this book.

Types of exhibition stand

Some companies invest in very large stands that are architectural in scale and may be built on several levels. Other stands are more sculptural or theatrical in approach but are 'bespoke', which means they are specially built by design rather then using 'off the shelf' components.

The overall success of the stand is dependent on its scale and visibility, the quality of its hospitality, the ability of its exhibits and giveaways to attract and also the skill of competitors to distract potential visitors. However, it is the creative skills of the exhibition designer that will ultimately dictate how the stand will work as a successful piece of communication, telling an engaging and persuasive story of the brand. From the exhibitor's perspective, achieving a measureable return on their investment is the bottom line. This might mean increased sales, improved brand recognition or an expansion of the market.

= **NORTH AMERICAN INTERNATIONAL AUTO SHOW**
COBO Center Detroit, Michigan, US

DATE
= **2010**

This image illustrates the scale of public exhibitions attended by thousands of visitors.

What is an exhibition?   Museum galleries

= **PITT RIVERS MUSEUM**
Oxford, UK

General Augustus Pitt Rivers donated his anthropological collection to the University of Oxford in 1884 and the Pitt Rivers Museum has now come to symbolise a way of collecting and display that seems part of a long dista past. Pitt Rivers was most interested in the design and evolution of human culture and his collection is a fascinati eclectic mix of objects, arranged thematically according to how objects were used, rather than their age or origin.

Museums are responsible for the storage, conservation, research and interpretation of our cultural heritage. Most importantly for exhibition designers, they are required to provide public access to collections. They vary in scale from state-funded national museums of international importance, to small subject-specific independent or privately owned museums. Museum collections represent all areas of human endeavour through time from collections of aircraft to butterflies; archaeology to nanotechnology. They are the storehouses of our collective material culture and a tangible link to the past.

A historical overview

Museums as we recognise them today have their roots in the Renaissance, when the wealthy and powerful gathered together strange, usually natural, objects in special rooms 'full of wondrous things', or more commonly, 'cabinets of curiosities'. Objects from the collections were grouped together into taxonomies, organised according to characteristics that linked them. To begin with this may have been arbitrary, for example, according to their size or even colour. However, as collections grew so too did the sophistication of their organisation and their contribution to scientific advancement. Collectors diversified to include archaeological and ethnographic objects as well as painting and sculpture. Works of art in particular developed a value that crossed national borders, giving them a currency of their own.

The industrialisation of Europe in the nineteenth century brought an expansion of museum building and new state-owned 'homes' for existing old collections. Just as the private collections symbolised the education, wealth and status of their owners, the now publicly owned collections, housed in grand neoclassical buildings, came to carry the same significance on behalf of a nation.

What is an exhibition?   Museum galleries

The modern museum

As the twentieth century progressed, the idea of the modern museum as a 'teaching machine' began to develop and by the 1970s there was an increasing realisation that museums needed to be more engaging. Interpretation led to more interactive learning as new ideas about how the museum could communicate, through dialogue and the construction of narratives, helped to generate 'a wealth of stories'. Museums became more open about their own fallibility and the need for community participation.

The millennium was a catalyst for the development of many new museums. It produced some iconic buildings that became landmarks; the Guggenheim played a crucial part in the regeneration of Bilbao in northern Spain, for example.

These new museums were audience-focused and ambitious in creating engaging, communicative learning experiences. The development of interpretation techniques was integral to these changes, and helped enable more effective ways of communicating the stories associated with museum collections. For example, consider an early twentieth-century silver cigarette case, an excellent example of its type, apart from an ugly gash in one corner. If displayed alongside a simple, descriptive label it could be exhibited as an object in its own right. However, if a letter written by its owner and his photograph is displayed alongside the object, telling the story of how it saved him from a bullet during the First World War, the 'dumb' object is transformed through a story of human experience, into a meaningful artefact that connects us with the past. As well as being storehouses of objects, museums are storehouses of memories.

The modern museum has a vital role in education and research, but also has to have relevance and appeal to modern audiences. Competition with a range of other leisure activities, from football to shopping, has led to a need for different ways of reaching an audience. The psychological approaches of creative advertisers are more in evidence as museums develop their own brand. Labels and panels covered in text are used less and an array of multimedia techniques are now employed to convey not only information, but also an interactive experience.

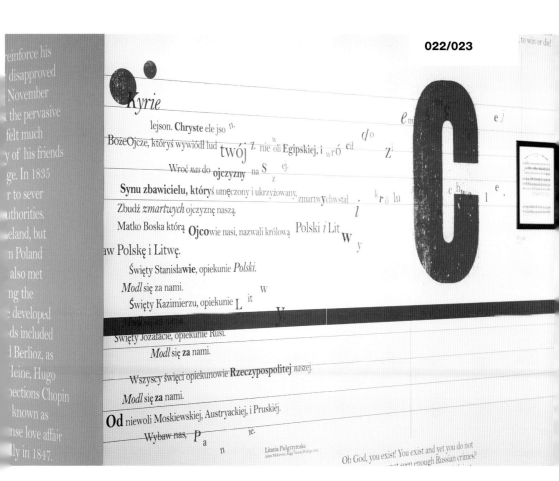

= **CHOPIN 200TH ANNIVERSARY EXHIBITION, BRITISH LIBRARY**
London, UK

DESIGNER
= **CHECKLAND KINDLEYSIDES**

DATE
= **2010**

Throughout the twentieth and twenty-first centuries, the idea of the modern museum as a 'teaching machine' has given rise to more engaging, interactive exhibitions. The Chopin exhibition at the British Library marked the 200th anniversary of the composer's birth and is a celebration of his life's work. By creating a graphic backdrop to the exhibition, using the symbols of sheet music and rhythmic typographic patterns, Chopin's story is brought to life and the passion and movement found in his music is portrayed effectively.

What is an exhibition? Museum galleries

= **ETHNOGRAPHIC
COLLECTIONS AT THE
QUAI BRANLY MUSEUM
Paris, France**

The ethnographic collection at Quai
Branly represents objects made
from a range of vulnerable materials.
Fabrics and paint pigments may
fade following too much exposure to
light, iron will rust in the presence of
air and moisture, wood will swell if
there is too much moisture but will
crack if the environment is too dry.
As a result, light, temperature and
humidity levels need to be carefully
controlled using specialist
conservation equipment.

Caring for collections

Museums are responsible for the curatorial care of their collections to make sure they are preserved for future generations.

This is what distinguishes museums from other 'types' of exhibition and it is the content of these collections that determines the nature of the museum. A collection of buses and trams, for example, will have different curatorial requirements from those for a collection of fans, and the way these collections are preserved will be determined by the nature of the materials they are made from.

When developing museum exhibitions, it is essential that the designer develops an understanding of the special requirements of valuable objects and works closely with the curator and other museum staff to ensure these issues are addressed effectively. Similarly, the nature of materials to be used in the construction of displays may have the potential to harm objects. For example, medium density fibreboard is a commonly used exhibition material, but needs to be formaldehyde free to prevent damage to artefacts.

?

BACKSTAGE

Although exhibitions form the museum's public face, the area 'backstage' has a vibrant and busy life of its own. As well as curatorial office and administration spaces, there may be environmentally controlled storage, conservation and restoration labs, areas where artefacts can be packed and unpacked and areas for research.

Within these spaces there has to be adequate access to all levels via lifts separate from the public, access points for artefacts to be transported to and from the museum, security systems and conservation control systems. This sophisticated infrastructure supports the museum's function, but is often invisible.

Exhibit

Any organised combination of objects, information in graphic, typographic and audio-visual form, supporting structure, and enclosure or housing that is designed to communicate. A single module within an exhibition.

What is an exhibition? Heritage

All around us, there is evidence of human intervention in the landscape. A broken piece of Roman pottery found as treasure in a field, historic houses, and World Heritage Sites all form an important cultural link for us with the past. Similarly, our wild, open landscapes help us to connect with the natural world and our place in the scheme of things. How can these sites be better understood and appreciated?

Visitor centres

The term 'visitor centre' describes an environment that can be used as a springboard to enjoying a cultural, commercial or landscape experience. It may form part of an existing building or be purpose built, but it is always a starting point from which visitors can orientate themselves both physically and emotionally while visiting the historical site.

Visitor centres help to manage visitor behaviour on a number of levels. The first concern is to provide for basic physical and practical needs. On another level, visitor centres can inform and educate the public about their visit in order to influence them in a positive way. This may be, for example, explaining the history of a site through exhibition, or how to behave in order to protect an area of outstanding natural beauty. In the case of a brand experience, supporting information underpins how visitors connect with a brand.

Successful visitor centres use an array of communication techniques, including interactive exhibitions, to help visitors move on to the next part of their visit feeling refreshed, enlightened and confident that they are heading in the right direction.

= **WHITBY ABBEY VISITOR CENTRE**
Whitby, UK

DESIGNER
= **STANTON WILLIAMS**

DATE
= **1998**

Occasionally, visitor centres are separated from a site, or may form part of less important outbuildings. At Whitby Abbey, the visitor centre has been sensitively created in a building of historic significance on site and views of the abbey can be seen through the windows. In this way, the integrity of the site is protected. Many historic buildings are situated within an equally important historic landscape or garden and a visitor centre may serve both.

Historic sites

From the archaeological layers of history in the ground beneath our feet to castles, stately homes, historic palaces, historic towns and buildings of religious significance, there are rich and engaging stories to tell relating to our cultural heritage. Most countries have established organisations for protecting sites of historic significance, which are involved in issues of archaeological conservation, restoration and interpretation. Through story-telling exhibitions that support the main site, visitor centres provide a useful mechanism for raising awareness and engendering a collective sense of ownership of our heritage.

What is an exhibition? Heritage

A gateway to the landscape

Visitor centres can also be found in protected natural landscapes of significance such as nature reserves, national parks and sites of special scientific interest (SSSI). They are usually owned and run by local or national bodies and often have a strong educational remit. As a result there are usually facilities for school groups and workshop activities that link to the theme of landscape. This type of centre will include information about identification and protection of flora and fauna and give advice about dealing with the challenges of a wild landscape.

Orientation is of great importance and most centres provide maps and other paper-based information to help visitors understand and orientate their way through the landscape. The visitor centre may act as an information hub that interprets the landscape through the use of paper-based trails, mobile technologies or art in the landscape. The centre provides opportunities for organisations to communicate important environmental, sustainability and behavioural messages that ultimately will enable visitors to enjoy their experience and protect it for others.

The brand experience

When visitor centres are associated with a commercial company, they may also be referred to as a 'brand experience'. Commercial visitor centres of this type are usually attached to a centre of production or a corporate headquarters. Examples include factories, distilleries, potteries or nuclear power stations. The centre will form part of a wider experience that may include a visitor tour of the site and acts as an orientation for this experience. Visitors may learn about the history of a brand, the materials required to make products and where those materials are sourced. Stories about the people who work in the industry enable visitors to make human connections to difficult technical issues. This type of experience may also end in a visitor centre so that visitors can use basic facilities and enjoy refreshments but also, most importantly for the provider, visit the shop.

Just as in the case of a commercial exhibition stand, a commercial visitor centre or brand experience aims to present a consistency of values that will help to engender brand loyalty. Both in the visitor centre and as part of their visit opportunities are created to experience the brand, and in the case of a distillery or brewery, for example, this would include 'sampling' the product. Similarly there are opportunities for the visitor to develop a better understanding of the brand. This is a particular challenge for controversial industries such as nuclear or environmental technologies; where visitor centres offer opportunities to argue against the NIMBY (not in my back yard) attitude.

"Johnny"

= **EXHIBITION STAND FOR
JACK PURCELL AT PITTI UOMO
Florence, Italy**

DESIGNER
= **CHECKLAND KINDLEYSIDES**

DATE
= **2009**

For Jack Purcell's exhibition stand at
Pitti Uomo (a major international fashion
trade show), Checkland Kindleysides
designed a playful stand to reflect the
'sport and good-natured mischief of
the world champion badminton player'.

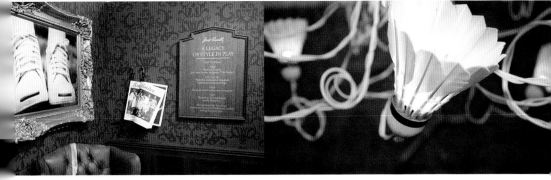

What is an exhibition? Art and leisure

Explicit communication is an important part of the exhibition designer's role; creating environments that convey messages that can be clearly understood by an audience. This section deals with creative approaches that lie at opposite ends of a spectrum of communication: on the one hand themed environments deal with explicit messages; art installations, on the other, may be more concerned with implicit methods.

= **SPLASH SCULPTURE**
WORLD EXPO 2008
Zaragoza, Spain

DESIGNER
= **PROGRAM COLLECTIVE:**
MONA KIM, TODD PALMER,
OLGA SUBIRÓS AND SIMÓN TAYLOR

DATE
= **2008**

Forming part of the 'Water for Life' exhibition, 'Splash' was a 22.5m (72ft) tall installation and acts as a metaphor for the arrival of water on the planet. It was formed from 84 independent and entirely computer-generated pieces. For the exhibition designer, installations require sensitivity and subtlety. The art must 'speak for itself' and visitors' responses will be personal and subjective.

Installation

Where art is involved, exhibition design tends to involve one or more of: artist, curator or designer. Their relationship is complex and the role of the exhibition designer is likely to be either invisible or absent. When designing an environment for painting, sculpture or other art works, it is important to respect the integrity of the work whilst enabling engagement for visitors. This requires sensitivity and subtlety; the art must 'speak for itself' in space. Unlike most of the communicative environments in which the exhibition designer works, here messages are implicit; the visitor engagement with the piece is an intimate one and visitors' aesthetic responses and sense-making are subjective and personal.

At first glance, installation art has many similarities with exhibition design. It is site specific, usually interior and three-dimensional, and it involves the transformation of the perception of space. Installations can be found in a range of public and private spaces including museums, art galleries and expos. They can also potentially share a wide variety of exhibition media including film, sound and light. Both disciplines have concerns for time and space, the sensory experiences of the audience and the idea of art as theatre. Designers and artists often work together to form very successful collaborations. The work of artists often adds variety and challenges the visitors, extending their cultural experience.

What is an exhibition? Art and leisure

= **DISNEYLAND PARK**
California, USA

DESIGNER
= **WALT DISNEY**

DATE
= **1955**

Themed environments are not 'real' but through theatrical effects and sometimes the use of actors, they create narrative experiences that the visitor can become fully immersed in. Disney parks and resorts are famous for the imaginative experiences they offer, described by Disney himself as 'dedicated to the ideals, the dreams, and the hard facts that have created America ...'.

Themed environments

Theming can be useful for conveying messages that are meant to be literal and straightforward and for creating enjoyable experiences for audiences who are enjoying leisure time.

Themed environments can be applied to any space. Obvious examples would be Disney stores and Planet Hollywood themed restaurants. Here film props are used with theatrical effect to 'dress' the space and simulate, compress and intensify experiences.

Like film sets, themed environments are not 'real' but recreate narrative experiences that seem familiar to their audiences and fulfil visitor expectation. They can be immersive and offer a temporary escape from reality, a 'suspension of disbelief', enabling visitors to journey into imaginary worlds.

Many historic recreations use theming as a vehicle to help bring history back to life for their audiences. For example, Sovereign Hill is an open-air museum in Ballarat in Australia, built on the site of an actual goldmine from the 1850s Australian gold-rush. There is a replica of the town housing, a range of attractions including shops, a theatre, and an opportunity to pan for gold and ride on a stagecoach. The use of actors, who have researched real historical characters, brings the whole experience to life. In this instance, there is a clear crossover between education and entertainment, an example of 'edutainment' where heritage meets theme park (see page 90).

: **WALT DISNEY**
To all who come to this happy place – welcome. Disneyland is your land. Here age relives fond memories of the past and here youth may savour the challenge and promise of the future. Disneyland is dedicated to the ideals, the dreams, and the hard facts that have created America ... with the hope that it will be a source of joy and inspiration to all the world.

Exhibitions are for people, so the exhibition designer needs to have an understanding of the physical, emotional and intellectual needs of a range of very different audiences in order to deliver environments that are accessible, educational and enjoyable. In order to understand how to communicate with an audience, the designer must have an understanding of how audiences learn and ways in which to facilitate this learning.

The design process begins with a thorough understanding of the constraints and opportunities offered by the brief. Once research has been completed and the storyline identified, the process of developing the exhibition within the space can begin.

Exhibition design Exhibition families

The term 'exhibition' has multiple definitions. For simplicity, the discussions that follow will use the umbrella terms 'commercial' or 'cultural' when describing a range of exhibition projects. Although most types of exhibition will fall loosely into one of these two categories, there will be an inevitable blurring of the boundaries between them.

The 'commercial' will broadly consider exhibitions that are telling the story of a brand or are predominantly engaged with issues relating to commerce. They include commercial exhibition stands, brand experiences, theme parks, theme retail interiors and leisure attractions. Many commercial exhibitions will charge entry or are only open to audiences who work is related to commerce. Whilst exp is also concerned with the promotion an better understanding of cultural relation their particular historical engagement w trade means that in this text they will be considered under the commercial bann

Museums, galleries, historic sites, landscape and heritage attractions will be broadly considered under the ter 'cultural' exhibitions. These types of exhibition relate to the collective materi culture of societies, whether this is a significant collection of art, a historic house, a palace or site, or a wayfinding visitor centre for a natural landscape. Here the activity of storytelling will mos often engage with history, conservatio preservation and education.

= **THE EXHIBITION DESIGN PROCESS**
As this diagram shows, through a constant process of feedback and evaluation, the exhibition designer will encounter six stages in the design process: analysis, idea, development, proposal, detail, installation. This approach was inspired by a travelling exhibition of Leonardo da Vinci's sketchbooks. The simple but engaging exhibition used a series of interpretive animations to bring the sketchbooks to life.

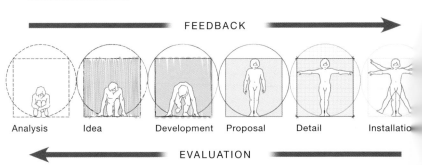

FEEDBACK

Analysis   Idea   Development   Proposal   Detail   Installatio

EVALUATION

The exhibition design process

The first step in becoming an exhibition designer is to develop an understanding of the design process. The diagram opposite has simplified this complicated process to a linear pathway that considers how a project moves from analysis to installation.

Exhibitions are designed for people. The figure in the diagram is a useful reminder that throughout the design process we should ask the question; what will be the nature of the physical and emotional relationship between the exhibition and its audience?

The circle represents all that is already known about the project; the client, the organisation, the site, a body of research that will create a story. The square represents the dialogue between the audience and the exhibition space.

The boundaries between analysis and concept design development are fluid and require constant feedback or return loops; testing and re-testing of ideas. Slowly the design will evolve to a point where a realistic proposal emerges for presentation to the client. Following input from the client team, the designer can begin to engage with the detail design process and the technical requirements of tendering. Installation forms the beginning of the end of the process. At each stage of the project there will be critical feedback, which at the end of the project takes the form of reflection on the whole in order to inform future projects.

? **IS AN AGRICULTURAL SHOW A 'CULTURAL' OR 'COMMERCIAL' EXHIBITION?**
It is an opportunity for exhibition, competition and performance. It is an opportunity to educate, stimulate and entertain. It has collections of farm animals and farm equipment. It is an important annual meeting place for farming communities.

Exhibition design The role of the exhibition designer

The specialist role of the exhibition designer is to create a three-dimensional environment that tells a story. This may be about a collection, a brand or simply an idea. Exhibition designers use a range of media and technologies, often borrowed from other disciplines, in order to effectively communicate messages in space.

The organised creative

As in other creative areas, exhibition designers need to be highly computer literate and require a varied two- and three-dimensional digital and analogue skills set.

However, it is the ambition to generate clear explanations to exhibition audiences, coupled with a focus on interior communicative content, which makes the exhibition designer distinct from designers in other disciplines.

The client is interested in their specialist expertise to create an exhibition according to an agreed set of communication requirements. It is the responsibility of the designer to identify, clarify and communicate these needs within the creative team.

As professional practitioners, exhibition designers need to work to deadlines, manage budgets, have an understanding of legal, access and sustainability issues, and possess a range of design, management and interpersonal skills that are pivotal to the creative team and influence the smooth running of a design project.

= **ROWING GALLERY,
RIVER AND ROWING
MUSEUM**
Henley-on-Thames, UK

DESIGNER
= **LAND DESIGN STUDIO**

DATE
= **1998**

The complex nature of many exhibition projects requires the designer to be an excellent communicator, negotiating not only with the client but often with a team of creative specialists. For their design of the galleries of the privately funded River and Rowing Museum, Land Design Studio had to work closely with architects, researchers, graphic designers and specialist contractors.

Exhibition design The role of the exhibition designer

= **S1NGLETOWN,
VENICE ARCHITECTURE BIENALLE**
Venice, Italy

DESIGNER
= **KESSELSKRAMER AND DROOG**

DATE
= **2008**

As part of the 2008 Venice Bienalle, KesselsKramer and Droog were asked to create S1NGLETOWN, an exploration of single living. Sources predict that by 2026, a third of the population of the developed world will be 'single', living apart from the traditional family unit. The implications of this shift are explored by this exhibition – visitors can walk the streets of S1NGLETOWN, visit its citizens and 'discover the technology, designs and services that might contribute to a single-oriented urban space of tomorrow'. An accompanying newspaper also features an in-depth exploration of single living.

Analysing the brief

All design projects begin with a thorough analysis of the 'project brief'. This will form the agreed foundation on which to build the project. As all projects are unique, briefs vary in detail and content according to the project's nature and scale, as well as the experience of the client. In the fast turnover of the commercial world, a brand manager may write briefs on a regular basis, but for the client of a new museum the project may be a 'one-off'. It is only through clear dialogue, to tease out detailed aims and expectations, that the brief can be fully understood. Essential initial questions include:

What is the nature and purpose of the project?

What is the scale of the project?

Who is the target audience and what are their needs?

Who is the client team?

What is the context and position of the site?

What is the budget?

What is the timescale?

The answers to these questions will generate a dialogue with the client. For example, they may establish the specific requirements relating to the brand or collection. The brief will also dictate the specific expertise that will be required in the design team from the start. Following discussion, negotiation and alteration, the brief will become the basis on which a contract is drawn up.

Once the project starts, the brief will become the designer's constant companion and point of reference. It is the key document that links the designer with the client and is the foundation of this relationship.

Exhibition design Exhibition space

Having read and understood the brief and its requirements, the design team will, if possible, make a site visit in order to clearly understand its overall context.

= **SPLAT, REINVENTING GRAND ARMY PLAZA**
New York, USA

DESIGNER
= **PENTAGRAM**

DATE
= **2008**

Careful consideration of the site is a crucial part of the design process. Exhibitions can even be designed for the outdoors, such as this one in New York, USA. Here, Pentagram were asked to produce an exhibition of 30 proposals for a 'reinvention' of Grand Army Plaza – a vast urban space in central New York. The proposals were displayed on fourteen 2.5m (8ft) cubes and two triple-height cubes arranged around the centre of the plaza. 'Their placement on the site allows visitors to more closely imagine what it would be like for any of these proposals to be implemented.'

Working with a site

For an exhibition within an existing building there will be many practical questions that need to be asked. Is the building listed and if so what are the restrictions regarding intervention in the space? Is there sufficient access to bring objects and exhibits into the space? Is the floor strong enough to receive exhibits or will it need to be reinforced to support heavy objects? Is there access to services? How will media run? Does space need to be made within the exhibit for storing support equipment for exhibition media? Are there existing obstacles to consider – columns or changes in level, for example?

Reference to existing plans, elevations and sections will give the designer an understanding of the scale, the available floor space, window and other heights, services, entrances and exits, mezzanine levels, internal stairs, lifts and a host of other considerations that will influence the design right from the start. If technical drawings do not exist, the design team may need to carry out an accurate site survey, measuring the sizes and key components of all the related structures.

Exhibition design Exhibition space

= **THE GREAT HALL,
NATIONAL RAILWAY MUSEUM
York, UK**

The artefacts in York's Railway Museum
are not only historically significant, but
many are awkwardly large and very heavy.
Specialists are required to move these
objects and will need to know from the
designer and curator exactly where they
are to be placed early in a design scheme.

Orientation
Wayfinding, informing visitors by way of signposts, maps, and trails,
where they are, and where they are going.

= **AN EMPTY HALL AT EXCEL**
London, UK

At the start of a commercial exhibition project, the 'site' only exists on plan. At this point, the actual venue is an empty void.

What is the context of the new exhibition within the existing building? The designer will need to consider how to design a transition space for visitors entering and leaving the space. For larger sites, how will visitor flow be managed? Are there views to the outside that may influence the orientation of the exhibition? What is the journey from the car park to the exhibition? Where are the facilities? How will the visitors' experiences be managed?

Most major cities throughout the world offer purpose-built exhibition halls that, in essence, are vast empty voids waiting to be filled with exhibition paraphernalia.

The exhibitor's manual will provide rules and regulations about stand heights, access to services, use of materials and the ability to hang lighting rigs from the roof. All this information will inform the heights required for branding, sight-lines from entrances, visitors' flow and access, all of which will, in turn, influence design decisions and help maximise the impact of the brand.

Whatever the nature of the exhibition, a thorough understanding of the site provides an envelope in which the design team can work, a context for consideration and, on occasion, inspiration.

? **SIMPLICITY AND FLEXIBILITY**
The designer of a travelling international exhibition has much to consider: different venues; a range of languages; security, transport and insurance issues; knowledge of services, lighting and existing context; cultural and religious understanding. These variables make the task complicated. Simplicity and flexibility are the key.

Exhibition design Designing for people

main consumers of education: the pupils themselves.
They are given the role of clients, and form teams
to create a design brief to resolve an issue in their
school. A designer or architect is appointed to work

and together they engage in a process that
leads to innovative design concepts for schools.

After 7 years of development involving 100 schools,
700 pupils in client teams and 10 000 pupils overall,
joinedupdesignforschools has generated a list of
common issues that pupils want to address.

This exhibition highlights these common issues, and
shows some of the concepts that have been created
by designers in response to the brief from their pupil
client teams, including a number that have been
implemented with support from the DFES.

WHAT DO PUPILS LEARN?

At the heart of the joinedupdesignforschools
programme is the development of pupils' life skills.
By giving them the responsibility of being clients,
of being their school's representatives and decision-
makers, the pupils acquire work and social skills
that are invaluable for their future. And, as they see
their involvement taken seriously, the pupils' self-
confidence and self-esteem grows.

teamwork

SOCIAL SPACES

SOCIAL SPACES

Whether an exhibition is culturally or commercially focused, the primary role of the exhibition designer is to create environments within which communication with an audience can take place.

= **YOUNG DESIGN CENTRE**
London, UK

DESIGNER
= **CASSON MANN**

DATE
= **2007**

A thorough analysis of the audience will be at the centre of good exhibition design. Here, Casson Mann were asked to design an exhibition for the Young Design Centre, to appeal to both younger and older audiences. Old wooden desks (some containing touchscreens, films and an inviting light that flickers, even when the desk lid is shut) were used to house the exhibition content. These desks behaved in a less orderly fashion as the exhibition progressed from the history of schooling to the modern-day, adding a sense of playfulness that appealed to both adults and children.

Who is the audience?

Audience analysis will start by questioning the nature of the audience. Is the exhibition expected to attract predominantly individuals, couples, families, national or international tourists or subject specialists and educational groups that may include school children or a combination of the above? Will there need to be special consideration of visitors' age, gender, race or physical and emotional ability? Will visitors be attending in their leisure time, or as part of their work? Will the exhibition aim to appeal to a wide audience, or will it focus on a specific group?

Families will need spaces that can facilitate small groups of people hoping for a collaborative experience. They will require a hierarchy of information that is of interest to a range of age groups and learning abilities. Children's exhibitions will require specialist design decisions regarding height, size, colour and use of materials. The age group will dictate their literacy levels and will influence how they engage intellectually. Children require the use of appropriate language, font choices and images, and tend to respond positively to interactive environments.

In contrast, a specialist audience will require a greater depth of information, supported by additional written material that can be accessed as a book or online.

For international audiences, all the above parameters apply, with additional considerations relating to culture and language.

Exhibition design Designing for people

Measuring audiences

As well as their cultural and emotional needs, audiences come in a range of different shapes and sizes. Anthropometric study provides us with knowledge about the dimensions of the human body and what it means to be 'average'. This has a direct relationship with the measurements of all exhibition elements, from furniture to graphics. Ergonomics is the study of human interaction with space and how the design of space influences how people operate in it. Can visitors pass comfortably? Are there clear safe routes to fire exits?

Exhibition spaces are never passive. When visitors are invited to physically interact with exhibition space they become performers within it. The designer needs to ensure that the design can accommodate the physicality of this performance. A combined understanding of anthropometrics and ergonomics helps the designer to create comfortable and user-friendly environments.

? **MEASURE OF MAN**

The study of anthropometrics was popularised by Henry Dreyfuss in 1960 with his book *The Measure of Man*. The book featured the 'average' measurements of Joe and Josephine and encouraged the idea that all design problems should be related to the human figure. A general source of ergonomic information is *The New Metric Handbook* which helpfully deals with the measurements required for most human environments.

As well as individual scale, designers need to consider how to manage audiences en masse. Wait times within exhibitions need consideration and audio-visual presentations should not be longer than three to five minutes or visitors either at worst get bored or at best cause a bottleneck.

Information about expected visitor numbers impacts on visitor management and flow to enable the best possible engagement and experience. Large visitor throughput, as experienced at an expo, requires effective queue management. An effective designer will consider as part of their design strategy how visitors will be entertained while they wait, in order to evoke a sense of anticipation that is fulfilled on their arrival.

= **ANTHROPOMETRIC MEASUREMENTS**

Anthropometric study provides the exhibition designer with knowledge of the dimensions of the human body and what it means to be 'average'.

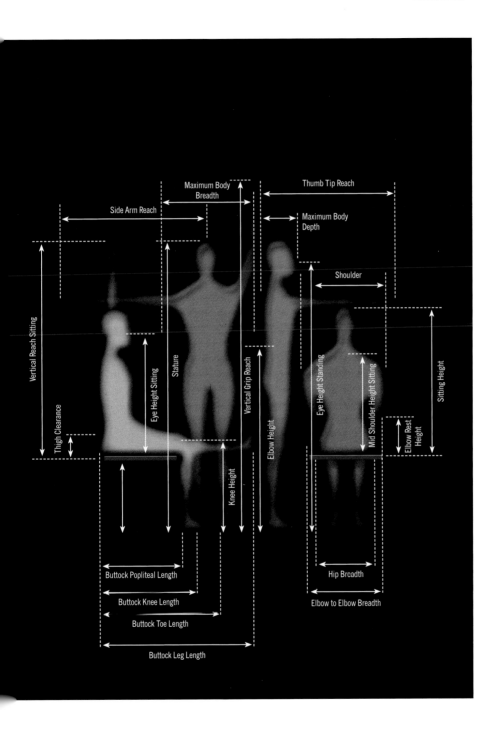

Exhibition design Designing for people

Access for all

Designing for access is an international concern that should enhance a visit for all audiences. An ethical designer should consider access as an established design habit, as well as a legal requirement, whereby access is considered at every stage of the design process.

When designing exhibitions the designer needs to consider visitors with mobility, hearing and visual impairments as well as those with learning disabilities who may experience intellectual barriers.

Physical access is not only about wheelchair users. Families with pushchairs and all those who find level changes difficult appreciate the opportunity to use a slope. Surfaces should be non slip and non trip, and deep gravel is a particular menace for those 'on wheels'.

Inside the exhibition, ask whether there are suitable turning places and sufficient distance between exhibits for a wheelchair and carer? Care must be taken to avoid designing exhibit elements that may create unnecessary obstacles and the design should allow for enough opportunities for visitors to sit down. An exhibition on multiple floors will need a lift; however, thought should be given to how the position of the lift and the orientation of the 'story' relate to each other, so that lift users are not disadvantaged.

Thoughtful consideration of heights can enrich experience, whether this is the height of furniture, interactive exhibits, display cases or graphical information. For visitors with a sensory deficit, whether this is sight or hearing, the imaginative use of other sensory experiences such as touch, taste and smell offer another layer of communication for all visitors.

For those with hearing difficulties, induction loops make a significant difference and sound showers help to focus the sound in specific areas, which reduces sound spill. Similarly the use of hard and soft materials has a significant effect on audio quality in space.

Engaging audio tours are of great value to everyone, and supporting written and visual material enables those with hearing difficulties to access the same information. The most appropriate language for audiences should be used and specialist copywriters are required for this.

It should not be underestimated how much the physical and emotional comfort of visitors affects the quality of their visit. Basic needs such as toilets and refreshments are obvious, but will only found through clear signage. Orientation signage, diagrammatic exhibition plans and maps give visitors a sense of the scale of an exhibition, will help with wayfinding and enable visitors to make judgements about the length of their stay in each area.

It is only after visitors feel comfortable confident in an environment that they will be ready to move onto a higher level of engagement that involves learning.

Understanding audiences

All audiences will bring different physical, practical, cultural, emotional and educational needs to an exhibition and this will influence how they learn.

As human beings, we all have a range of emotional and cultural experiences that inform our understanding of the world and how it works. Everyone forms a complicated and interrelated collection of memories that are unique, built over years of experience. An analogy is to think of an imaginary mental landscape that we build for ourselves. When we are young, the topography is limited, but as we mature, we are continually adding vast amounts of detail, from single blades of grass to huge buildings; all connected in some way to our personal landscape. By adulthood the landscape is incredibly complex and impossible to see all at the same time. However, we know that with prompting from navigational signposts, we can seek out the information we need to underpin understanding. It is within this unique memory landscape of experience that we add new knowledge and construct the next layer of our learning.

IMPLICIT AND EXPLICIT MESSAGES
Exhibition designers are mainly concerned with delivering 'explicit' messages that audiences can easily understand. 'Implicit' messages are more subjective and open to interpretation. Which of the following are concerned mainly with explicit or implicit messages: an art gallery, a theme park or a brand experience?

: **KATHY RAYWORTH**
Accessibility enables everybody to function in the most independent and natural way possible. Creating environments that are accessible does not compromise design, it enhances it.

How can these ideas be applied to learning in exhibitions? Semiotics is the study of the way in which signs and symbols can act as catalysts for a string of thought processes. Everything we see signifies something for us based on what we have previously learnt about the world. This relates directly to how we understand the visual and material culture we have constructed in our memory landscape.

In Western societies, it is traditional for a bride to wear white to signify purity and new beginnings. However, in India, white is symbolic of death, and an Indian bride will dress in red. Similarly, in China red signifies 'love'. In the West, red signifies stop or danger. Everything from the colours to the language we use signifies information in subtly different ways to different cultural audiences. These ideas have been used by advertising agencies for years to encourage us to buy goods. For example, a bottle with a red and white label may subliminally remind us of Coca Cola. Similarly, if goods are associated with lifestyles to which we aspire, we may be encouraged to buy them.

Exhibition design Understanding the story

= **PHILIPPINES PAVILION
WORLD EXPO 2008
Zaragoza, Spain**

DESIGNER
= **ED CALMA**

DATE
= **2008**

The overall theme of Expo 2008 in Zaragoza
was 'Water and Sustainable Development'.
The design of the pavilion aimed to raise
awareness of rising sea levels, which are
of particular concern to the people of the
Philippines. The interior of their pavilion
featured a series of large 'bubbles' carrying
messages. The blue lighting effects added
to the overall 'watery' environment.

Whether an exhibition is about a collection, an idea or a brand, the exhibition designer needs to clearly understand what the client hopes to achieve from the exhibition. What is its purpose and how will the messages communicated by the exhibition leave its audience changed?

WALLY OLINS
...to be really effective you have to be able to sense the brand. You may even be able to touch it and feel it. So that it manifests the core idea.

Cultural and commercial messages

In considering exhibition objectives, let us consider two very different types of exhibition with similar themes. The first is about recycling, a temporary exhibition at a science museum called 'Wash 'n' Squash', and the second is a commercial exhibition stand at a public environment show for a company that sells 'Ewash', a non-toxic, wildlife-friendly washing power.

Cognitive objectives relate to the important information we want the audiences to learn about recycling and 'Ewash'. Research has suggested that on average audiences leave an exhibition with six new pieces of information. In these two scenarios how would the six key messages be effectively communicated?

Emotional objectives address how we want our audiences to feel as a result of their visit. Visitors to 'Wash 'n' Squash' have played with a series of interactives about recycling supported by family centred graphics, and so feels positive and motivated. The evocative wildlife imagery of the 'Ewash' stand has made the audience feel good about a brand that is helping to look after natural habitats.

Behavioural objectives consider how visitors may change their behaviour as a result of their exhibition experience. Have the exhibitions influenced our respective audiences to make more of an effort to recycle or change to using environmentally friendly cleaning products? Clearly, if this is the case, the exhibitions have been successful in their proposed aims and objectives.

Exhibition design Understanding the story

Communicating the story

Interpretation is a communicative process that uses a range of media to help audiences to understand information. It is not 'what' you interpret, but how you interpret it. When delivered effectively, it is a mechanism that helps audiences to be surprised, inspired and curious to learn more.

The most effective interpretation is provocative rather than instructional, encouraging audiences to ask questions about what they have learned. Audiences will understand more when they can relate information to their own experience and understanding of the world, and as a result stories about people are much more empathic. When information is revealed through interpretation, particularly when this is difficult information that the visitors do not believe they will ever be able to understand, the revelation is often a 'eureka' moment that cannot help but affect them.

When we talk about quantities, for example, it is much easier to remember a large expanse of land as being equivalent to so many 'football pitches'. Similarly we have a far better cognitive sense of the weight of a large object, if it is measured in an equivalent number of elephants. Similarly, when information is understood using imaginative connections, visitors are more likely to remember it. Through interpretation, abstract measures and ideas can be translated into something that the visitor can connect to and understand from their own life.

The exhibition designer can help facilitate this process by helping the client to build an interpretive bridge between the experts on the one hand, and the public on the other, posing as the 'interested layman'. The foundations of this bridge lie in the mix of appropriate language and exhibition media that help to PROVOKE, RELATE and REVEAL information to the audience. Through the interpretation process, environments can be created that are not only engaging and enlightening, but also enjoyable.

: **FREEMAN TILDEN**
Any interpretation that does not somehow relate what is being displayed or described to something within the personality or experience of the visitor will be sterile.

= **NATIONAL HOLOCAUST EXHIBITION, IMPERIAL WAR MUSEUM**
London, UK

DESIGNER
= **AT LARGE**

DATE
= **2000**

This display cabinet of shoes is an emotive use of very personal objects. Each shoe is a relic of terrible human suffering and when displayed en masse can make profound human connections for visitors.

= **INTERNATIONAL SLAVERY MUSEUM**
Liverpool, UK

DESIGNER
= **REDMAN DESIGN**

DATE
= **2007**

The slavery museum acts as a powerful reminder from history. It is shocking yet emotive and has pertinent messages about racial tolerance in the twenty-first century.

Exhibition design Understanding the story

= **THE COLLECTION**
Lincoln, UK

DESIGNER
= **EVENT COMMUNICATIONS LTD**

DATE
= **2005**

For this exhibition, Event Communications Ltd took a chronological approach to the storyline. The exhibition cleverly moves visitors through time by arranging displays chronologically around the perimeter of the exhibition. A 'timeline' hung as a graphic helps visitors to historically orientate themselves and the central area enables visitors to break away from this chronological route as they choose.

Organising the story

The search for a logical and engaging storyline requires thorough research of the subject matter. This process may generate a volume of text and visual information, which at first may appear random and at times overwhelming. Articulating information diagrammatically is a useful way to identify possible themes and routes of enquiry. Bubble and spider diagrams are enormously helpful for seeing connections between ideas whilst maintaining an overview of the information. (See pages 58–59.)

For the designer, as a visual thinker, key themes and subtopics will gradually emerge from the diagrammatic clutter as ideas slowly become more organised.

Throughout this process, concept ideas may emerge and should be captured quickly through sketching and note taking, before they sink back into complicated threads of information.

At every stage, make reference to the brief and its aims and objectives: What is the story about and who is it for? What are the most important parts of the story that the storyteller wants the audience to remember? What are the limitations of the space and budget? What is the clearest and most appropriate way to communicate messages?

As an understanding of the material develops, key ideas and subtopics begin to emerge from the organised chaos, settling into collective themes like the chapters of a book. There is a gradual distillation of the most important information that can then be organised into a logical hierarchy.

?

INFORMATION GATHERING
Research suggests that people remember:
Ten per cent of what they read
Twenty per cent of what they see
Fifty per cent of what they hear and
Ninety per cent of what they do

How might this influence exhibition design?

Storyline
A written description of the narrative content of an exhibition or event.

Exhibition design Student case study

PROJECT
= THE STORY OF TEA

DESIGNER
= JESSE KU

DATE
= 2004

= Sketches can help by serving as visual 'notes to self' alongside organisational diagrams.

! For this project, students were asked to develop designs for an exhibition telling the story of tea. A variety of techniques were used to organise the narrative and develop a clear storyline. A complex mind map explores the fascinating subject of tea, looking at its history, where it is grown and its cultural importance. At this stage of the project the designer has to mentally juggle a number of ideas and concentrate hard not to lose important threads.

Once the storyline is clear, the mind map becomes simpler. It is useful to start dropping it into a simple plan as a series of 'blobs'. This initiates the relationship of the story to the space that signals the start of the physical design.

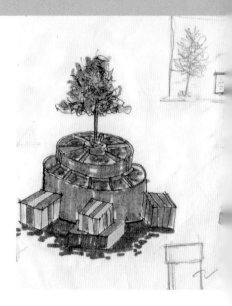

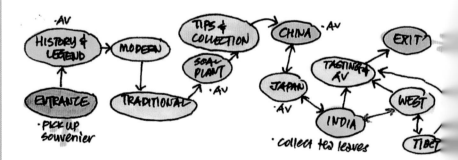

= As the storyline becomes clear, the mind map becomes simpler.

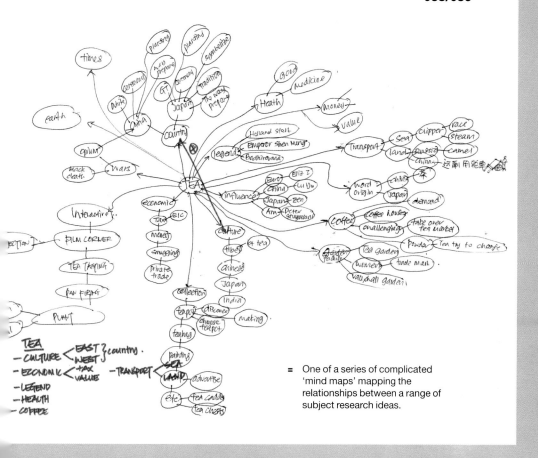

= One of a series of complicated 'mind maps' mapping the relationships between a range of subject research ideas.

? Now imagine you have been invited to tell the story of your life as an exhibition.

1 Draw a spider diagram that includes everything and everyone that has helped to shape your life.

2 Distil your diagram down to six key areas that represent the main themes you want to talk about.

3 Next to these themes, list all the topics you would want to cover in more detail.

4 As you develop ideas for your exhibition, add in little thumbnail sketches of these ideas alongside your diagram.

For the exhibition designer, the concept design phase signals the start of finding mechanisms to translate the 'story' into space, and this will take place through a series of 'conversations'.

They will have many 'private' conversations with their imagination, stirring up and connecting ideas that leap from problem to problem and back again. These complicated thought processes are externalised through a range of quickly drawn, two- and three-dimensional sketches; constantly thinking, questioning and re-evaluating problems. Gradually, having played with various ideas and rejected some, the restless and apparently disjointed concepts begin to settle into a possible solution that may be feasible.

At this stage a more public conversation is possible with the client, translating ideas into a visual form that can be clearly understood. Whilst ideas will continue to refer back to research and the brief, the client presentation is the basis for the project 'proposal'.

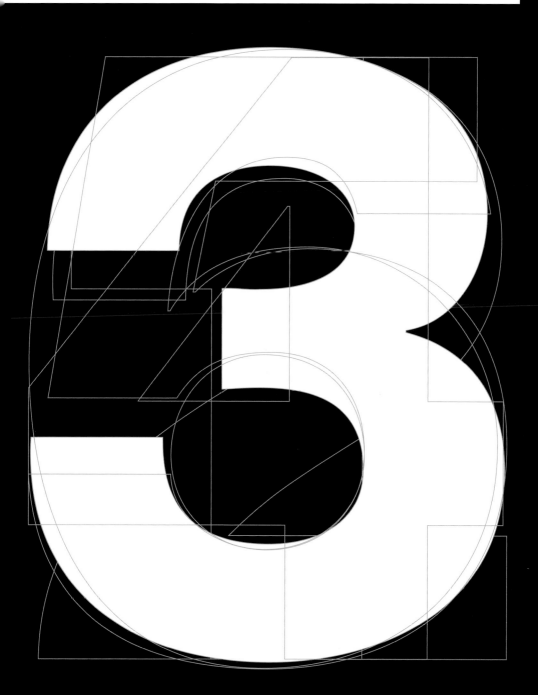

Designing a narrative Inspirational triggers

Every exhibition is different with a unique set of problems to be solved within the constraints of the brief. At the concept stage of the design process, the designer is seeking inspirational triggers that will help to generate creative, imaginative ideas. But where do creative ideas come from?

= **HARRODS SHOP WINDOW**
London, UK

At Christmas in particular, shop windows often become small exhibitions in their own right. Harrods in London, UK, took advantage of the fiftieth anniversary of the film *The Wizard of Oz* to theme its windows. Each told a different part of the story, whilst introducing merchandise from the store.

Brainstorming

Creative ideas cannot be formed in a vacuum and thorough research to support an exhibition is a good starting point. 'Blue sky thinking' or 'brainstorming' is a valuable technique used by creatives to seek inspiration and enables the collective experience of the participants to play a part. By bouncing ideas off each other, the designer hopes to generate a catalyst that will trigger creative thought processes. In itself, successful brainstorming can only take place within a relaxed environment of mutual trust and respect. Discussion and argument should never be personal and though potentially passionate, should be good natured. Humiliation serves only to strangle any hope of free expression.

Brainstorming sessions for designers usually include large pieces of paper, mark makers, endless supplies of coffee and much stretching and pacing about! Successful sessions will lead to the distillation of a range of possible ideas for the designer to take forward. Similarly, looking at the work of other artists and designers in a range of disciplines may be useful, particularly when trying to identify where to 'pitch' a project in terms of current design trends.

Visual research

As visual thinkers, designers need to find ways of immersing themselves in inspirational information and environments. Thinking needs to be supported by rich visual and other sensory material. For example, collections of evocative images, colours or material samples can be brought together as mood or material boards. Inspiration may come from the objects in a collection or the goods supplied by a brand. Creating a mix of inspiration or mood boards helps to distil ideas and make them visible.

As part of this process the exhibition designer has a useful additional tool, 'theming'. Depending on the nature of the project, a theme can become a hook onto which the designer can hang their ideas. This should not encourage a literal approach; an exhibition stand for a washing machine company will not necessarily be successful if built from over-scale washing machine components. However the theme of cycles and turning within water may generate other interesting ideas.

?

TRANSLATION AND ABSTRACTION
'Translation' enables the designer to take the familiar and change it into something else. 'Abstraction' challenges us to consider the qualities of an object or idea apart from its concrete reality. To 'deconstruct' is to break down or dismantle an object or idea into its constituent parts. Any of these may be starting points for seeking design inspiration.

Designing a narrative   Structure of narrative space

Exhibition design is a complex process that has to be carefully choreographed in order for all the elements to work harmoniously together. Following thorough research and brainstorming, concepts will begin to form. Alongside these ideas, the design team will find it useful to consider an appropriate 'approach' to designing the narrative in space.

= **CITYSCAPE, ECOBUILD**
London, UK

DESIGNER
= **PATRICK COLLINS, CAPITA**
LOVEJOY AND CAPITA SYMON

DATE
= **2010**

Cityscape is an installation that aims t
raise awareness of the importance of
sustainable infrastructure. The structu
was intended to highlight potential an
innovation in 'Living Wall' technologie
The interiors encouraged visitors to
consider sustainable infrastructure vi
a series of multimedia presentations
produced by Natural England. Stand
at eight metres high the central stand
also formed an orientational 'highligh
for exhibition visitors.

A chronological approach

A chronological approach to designing an exhibition is useful when there is a significant timeline supporting the narrative, or an important order in which a story needs to be told, in order for it to make sense. The chronology becomes a vital support for the story from start to finish. The story of the famous nineteenth-century engineer Isambard Kingdom Brunel could be told through his amazing engineering feats: the Clifton suspension bridge in 1831; the network of tunnels, viaducts and bridges designed for the Great Western Railway, from 1833; and the *SS Great Britain* launched in 1843 – the world's first iron-hulled passenger liner.

However, a vital part of the story would be its relation to the extraordinary developments of the industrial age. The story would logically start Brunel's his birth in 1806 and would consider his childhood and family. This would be followed by threading through his career and achievements and would conclude with his early death in 1859 and the legacy of his life and creations.

Care has to be taken with a chronological approach, to avoid a rigid, linear experience that limits visitors to a single, specified route, forcing them through the exhibition in a rather mechanical fashion.

Designing a narrative Structure of narrative space

A thematic approach

A 'thematic approach' would employ the grouping of objects or ideas into a range of themes that could be viewed in any order. This enables a more open, free-flowing approach, whereby each theme within the overall story can be experienced independently. An exhibition about the five human senses would be a good example. It is unnecessary for there to be a specific order, each 'theme' having equal importance. However, with a thematic approach, the designer needs to take care to ensure that the audience still maintains an understanding of the story as a whole.

An 'integrated approach' is more commonly taken, where a combination of chronology and theme is used. The Isambard Kingdom Brunel exhibition may have a specific area on the theme of bridge building, but within this there is a very clear chronology indicating how the lessons learnt from each project fed into the next. Alongside these approaches, there may be island exhibits or synergetic displays which link to subthemes of the overall story.

A branded approach

A 'branded approach' puts brand identity at the core of the design and is an essential consideration for design decisions. The structure and form of the design is an opportunity to convey brand messages and should leave the audience in no doubt of the brand identity.

Observational research in museum environments suggests that visitors tend to move from left to right. The 'highlight approach' can take advantage of this behaviour by strategically placing objects or exhibits as a visually engaging 'pull' to help audiences move from one part of the exhibition to another. In the blockbuster exhibitions of recent years, this has been exemplified by artefacts with a 'star quality', for example Tutankhamun's death mask. For some visitors, these key objects are the main motivation for coming to the exhibition and they will seek them out. The challenge here is to persuade visitors to engage with the entire exhibition.

In a commercial environment, the 'highlight approach' will act as an 'attract' to pull visitors onto their stand and away from their competition. This could be anything from a climbing wall, a tower sculpted from sustainable materials, or the overall drama of the stand itself. Creating a sense of spectacle and excitement encourages visitors to engage. The exhibit become the focal point around which visitors can orientate themselves.

All these approaches help the designer to make decisions about how the space is planned and where key objects, exhibits or performance spaces will be placed. Alongside these decisions will be others about the use of exhibition media, how exhibits will relate to each other and their audience. As all of these complicated but interrelated issues are resolved, the overall design of the exhibition will begin to emerge.

? FORMS OF DISPLAY

Damien Hirst's diamond encrusted skull entitled 'For the Love of God' was displayed as part of a guest curated exhibition at the Rijksmuseum in Amsterdam in 2008. Strictly timed, visitors queued to be led though a series of short, dark tunnels that opened into a small black room. Centrally placed, the skull was housed in a simple glass case and lit from above. There followed an exhibition of art from the museum's collection, chosen by Hirst, about the representation of death in art. What are your thoughts about this approach to display?

= **THE HOUSE OF BOLS COCKTAIL & GENEVER EXPERIENCE**
Amsterdam, Netherlands

DESIGNER
= **'..., STAAT' CREATIVE AGENCY**

DATE
= **2007**

Throughout The House of Bols the visitor is reminded of the brand, its history and how it is made. The story is supported by interactivity, audio-visual displays and Bols artefacts. This image shows an area where visitors can smell different 'flavours' of Bols. The experience is great fun, ending with the opportunity to choose a Bols cocktail, which is made with a flourish by trained bar staff, in an intimate bar.

Designing a narrative Personal conversations

When presented with a design brief, the exhibition designer will begin by starting a series of 'personal conversations'. Here, ideas will be formulated, visualised, tested and developed using a number of techniques.

Keeping a sketchbook

There is much debate about the role, or even relevance, of drawing in an evermore sophisticated digital design environment. However, it is the analytical nature of drawing from life, which enables us to develop our visual understanding about how the world is made and fits together. The more we practise drawing, the more experienced we become in this understanding, creating for ourselves a valuable internal visual resource, which can be called upon when we need to solve design problems that only exist in the imagination. However, as we can only draw images based on what we already know, it is often useful to use visual reference to help us to draw accurately, to help us fill in the 'gaps' in our visual understanding.

Keeping a sketchbook enables the designer to continually practise a valuable and immediate technique that engenders credibility as a visual communicator. Sketching is not about perfectly finished images, but loose visual notes or marks that mean something. Their imperfection suggests further interpretation and dialogue, part of the design journey rather than its destination. The sketchbook can become a generic visual diary of enormous value for reference, but can also be a profoundly personal visual conversation with oneself.

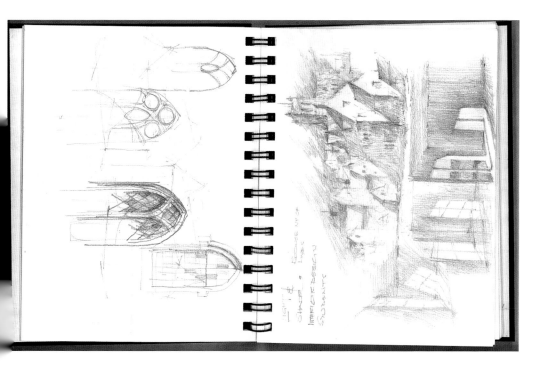

= **SKETCHBOOK**

DESIGNER
= **LEN RYE**

DATE
= **2009**

Len Rye has been an illustrator for more than half a century and has been a professional illustrator for exhibitions, museums and theatre. He keeps a sketchbook with him at all times to help his analysis of the world.

: **LEN RYE**
Drawing is a way of thinking.

? **DRAWING / REALITY**
In 1515 Albrecht Dürer drew a rhinoceros based purely on written description. Whilst it looks like a mythical beast, it is remarkable in its accuracy. The original drawing is owned by the British Museum. Sketch an elephant as accurately as you can from your imagination. Now look at photographic evidence; how does your drawing compare with reality?

Designing a narrative Personal conversations

Developing concepts

Following research and brainstorming, there may be a period of incubation to allow for ideas to develop in the imagination. The tangible and collaborative relationship between hand and eye, developed through drawing, remains a powerful and effective tool to help the designer to 'see' ideas. This visual conversation may continue over several sheets of paper. Overlaying transparent or tracing paper enables the designer to quickly trace ideas onto a fresh sheet whilst still sketching to scale.

The addition of colour is often helpful, as is highlighting a particular visual note as a future prompt. For some designers this visual conversation may start or indeed continue in three dimensions through sketch modelling. The use of recycled or reclaimed materials encourages free thinking and may even deliver serendipitous results.

Designers are problem solvers. This triangular relationship between hand, brain and eye facilitates a complex process of questioning and re-questioning. Frustratingly, there may be difficult periods of compromise, but gradually the vital pieces of the puzzle come together and solutions begin to surface.

: BRUNO MUNARI

The designer is the artist of today, not because he is a genius but because he works in such a way as to re-establish contact between art and the public, because he has the humility and ability to respond to whatever demand is made of him by the society in which he lives, because he knows his job, and the ways and means of solving each problem of design.

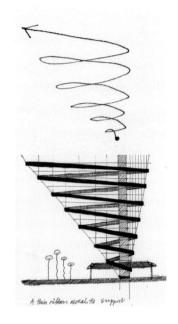

A thin ribbon reveals the support

= **THE VORTEX, PUERTO RICO PAVILION** Seville, Spain

DESIGNER
= **JOHN CSAKY**

DATE
= **1992**

These two development sheets form part of a set of five, where ideas for a 'vortex' styled exhibit for the Puerto Ri Pavilion were developed by John Csak All are dated 4.12.91, indicating that each sheet was developed on the sam day. As the designer's idea builds between sketches, he writes notes to himself about materials and possible media. Sketch elevations and a very simple figurative note help us to understand scale and scope within the space. The final exhibit was the centra piece of 'Puerto Rico Today' zone.

Designing a narrative Personal conversations

= This initial plan sketch indicates
   a first attempt at positioning the
   pods and exhibits.

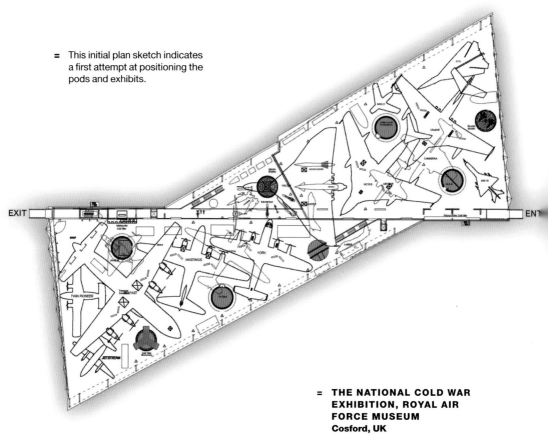

EXIT   ENT

= **THE NATIONAL COLD WAR
   EXHIBITION, ROYAL AIR
   FORCE MUSEUM**
   Cosford, UK

   DESIGNER
= **NEAL POTTER**

   DATE
= **2007**

   This exhibition was built to house a
   collection of post-World War II aircraft
   and Neal Potter was able to develop the
   exhibition concept before architects began
   their design work. This form of designing,
   from the inside out, meant that the building
   could be specifically built around the theme
   and the collection of post-World War II
   aircraft and the accompanying exhibition.
   'Hotspots' of interpretation at specific
   points in the space allow a degree of
   flexibility during the design process as
   'shuffling' of the aircraft would be inevitable.

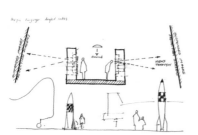

= Sections show how plans and elevations
   look when cut through, which allows interior
   structural features to be seen. As many
   exhibitions are situated in interior spaces the
   plan will actually be a plan section which is
   cut through at approximately head height.

= These images show how the interior of the pod developed from a very rough sketch into a collaged elevation, giving us an understanding of interior scale and graphics.

= The final image shows the finished pod. Note how little has changed in the design between the pod visual and the final exhibit.

Designing a narrative   Personal conversations

Scale and concept

At this stage of a project, the designer's most valuable tools are a pencil, a rubber, a scalpel and a scale rule. Although when sketching in two and three dimensions, the inclusion of a figure suggests a sense of 'how big' elements will be, quite quickly, the designer needs to work to scale, even if drawings are not completely accurate to the millimetre at this stage.

An object's actual size is 1:1, however when working with exhibitions it is impossible to draw the actual space at its real size. By drawing things to scale, we can draw very large objects to a manageable size. The most commonly used interior scales used by exhibition designers are 1:100, 1:50 and 1:20. When drawing the overall site 1:100 scale is most commonly used as it will usefully show the context of the exhibition. However, drawn at this scale there will be a limited amount of detail. A drawing at 1:50 is able to show much more detail of the exhibition because the proportions appear to be twice as big as those drawn at 1:100. If greater detail is required, the drawing can be repeated using a scale of 1:20.

When drawing exhibits at a furniture scale, the designer may work at 1:10 or 1:5, which will also give a clear indication of how graphic treatments will work. Only when a particular finish or fixing detail needs to be illustrated will a detail be drawn at 1:1. Scale is measured using a scale rule.

Orthographic drawings are measured to scale and show a plan, elevations and sections on the same sheet. Views are taken at right angles to each other. The plan indicates how a scheme will look when viewed from directly overhead. Elevations show how elements will look when viewed from the side. When drawing both plans and elevations the designer should draw without any interference from perspective. Plans, elevations, sections and details are a type of technical communication that will be considered in more detail later. However at the concept stage, their use, even in sketch form, enables the designer to keep within realistic spatial boundaries, which in turn feeds into the decision-making process.

Orthographic drawing
Measured scale drawing showing plan (or plan section) and elevations (or sectional elevations) on the same sheet. Views are taken at right angles to each other and presented in a conventional format.

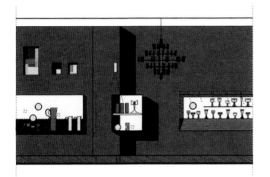
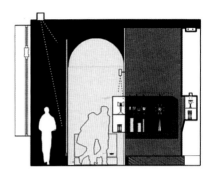

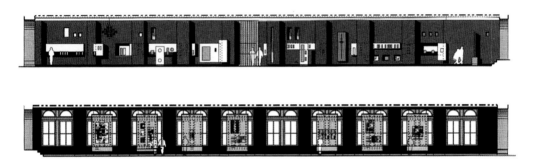

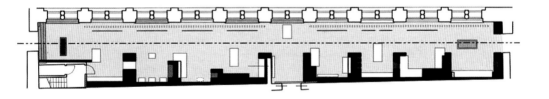

= **SACRED SILVER GALLERY,
VICTORIA & ALBERT MUSEUM**
(competition entry)
London, UK

DESIGNER
= **PROJECT ORANGE**

DATE
= **2003**

Even if drawings are not wholly accurate at
this stage, the inclusion of figures can help to
suggest scale and will give an idea of the size
at which design elements will appear.

Designing a narrative   Public conversations

Once the concept stage of a project is complete and the designer is content with 'the big idea' then a proposal will be generated for presentation to the client. A variety of techniques will be used in order for ideas and concepts to be communicated as clearly and as efficiently as possible.

Developing a proposal

Up until this point the designer has used a very personal design language, which may be difficult for non-designers to understand. The 'client presentation' requires a different type of communication that helps the client to clearly understand the proposal.

Clarity is paramount and the techniques chosen for presentation will vary between projects. They usually consist of a variety of two- and three-dimensional material, that may include hand-drawn sketch development work, full-colour visuals, rendered elevations, storyboards, client presentation plans, mood and material boards, models, supporting research images and written information explaining key ideas. Throughout, the inclusion of figures provides an immediate understanding of scale, and populated visuals bring a proposal to life.

Isometric drawings are a commonly used form of graphical projection. They are measured technical drawings that relate directly to plans and elevations and are drawn to scale, accurately illustrating the relationship of components of the three-dimensional exhibition in two dimensions. This enables the exhibition to be seen as a whole at a glance. When quickly sketched by hand, isometrics are also useful at the concept stage for generating a sense of three dimensions through drawing.

Rendered sectional elevations are a useful mechanism for communicating how a long section of space will look, and adding a figure gives a sense of scale.

Client presentation plans are commonly used as part of a presentation package to support other two- and three-dimensional work. Drawn accurately to scale they have a diagrammatic quality that is easier to 'read' than technical plans. Client presentation plans are usually in colour. They may show figures in plan, as well as all the key features of a scheme and arrows to show visitor orientation.

Isometric drawing
A drawing to scale such that each perpendicular axis is shown at 120° to the others.

Designing a narrative Public conversations

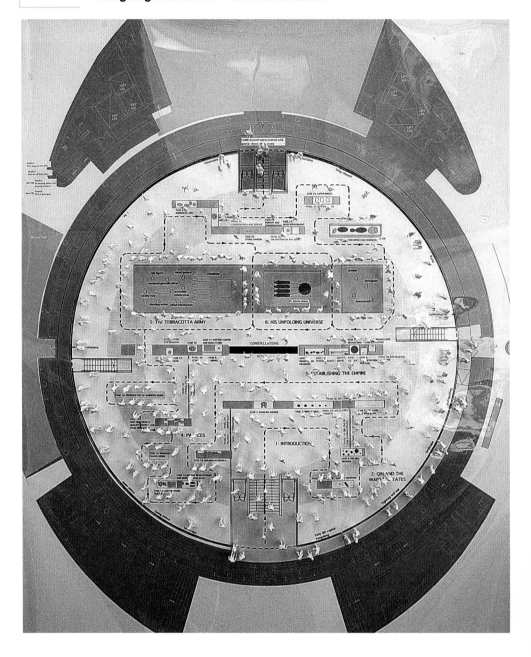

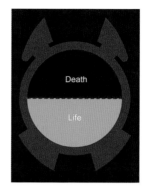

= **THE FIRST EMPEROR,
THE BRITISH MUSEUM**
London, UK

DESIGNER
= **METAPHOR**

DATE
= **2007**

When Metaphor were asked to convert
the Round Reading Room at the British
Museum into a temporary exhibition
gallery, they created a series of
drawings. Starting with an initial concept
drawing, these developed into design
drawings, showing layout and route,
presentation models, digital models
and three-dimensional drawings of
the space from above.

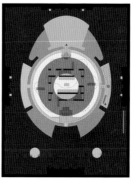

Designing a narrative Public conversations

= **CONCEPT MODEL FOR GRAND
STAIRCASE, THE GRAND
EGYPTIAN MUSEUM**
Cairo, Egypt

DESIGNER
= **METAPHOR**

DATE
= **2010**

Presentation models are invaluable as a
way of communicating the overall scheme
in three dimensions. A card model enables
the viewer to see the whole scheme at
once, indicating the relationship between
elements and clarifying visitor orientation.
This model gives us a sense of the huge
scale of the Cairo project, whilst the huge
artefacts become giant signposts or
'highlights' leading the visitor up to
different levels.

?

ANALOGUE OR DIGITAL
Hand drawing or computer generation?
What constitutes a design tool? Are the
pencil and the pixel mutually exclusive?

Visualisation and modelling

Designers need to avoid producing seductive plans that are meaningless in elevation. We experience the world from a three-dimensional perspective and realistically drawn visuals are the most accessible to the client. When generated from the spectator's eye-height, the view will answer the most eager of client questions, 'But what will it look like?'

Visuals can be produced by hand and rendered using a range of wet, dry and computer media, although markers remain a favourite for quick application. When scanned and digitally manipulated, hand-drawn images have the ability to add a unique personality and atmosphere to images. Generated in the computer, visuals can take advantage of digital lighting and rendering, creating realistic and convincing images.

Digital and analogue collage can produce persuasive images that create an 'impression' that still facilitates conversation with the client. Digital tablets facilitate a useful crossover between hand- and computer-drawn imagery.

The graphic-based content of exhibitions makes the use of colour models effective, as are computer-generated models. The versatility and relative cost of digital models has made them popular. In addition they can be animated (also called fly-throughs) creating the illusion that the viewer is able to walk through the space.

Designing a narrative Public conversations

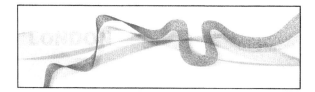

? **YOUR FIGURE**

It is useful to develop your own stylised figures to add to your personal and public conversations in two and three dimensions, as a visual reminder of human scale. Your figure should be simple, roughly in proportion and quick to draw.

Professional presentations

Computer literacy is an essential design skill. Professional presentations are usually given using presentation software, for example PowerPoint, but often presentation work needs to be seen by a range of different people and needs to translate easily to hard copy that can 'speak' for itself. These portfolios are often in A2 or A3 landscape format and include a range of other important material, from budgets to company information.

= **CAPITAL CITY PROJECT,
MUSEUM OF LONDON**
London, UK

DESIGNER
= **FURNEAUX STEWART DESIGN**

These presentation boards give a good
indication of how the space might look
on completion.

Designing a narrative Student case study

PROJECT
= **EXHIBITION STAND FOR
'MINI CONCEPT' AT
FRANKFURT MOTOR SHOW**

DESIGNER
= **MELISSA PEARCE**

DATE
= **2010**

= The ribbon theme conveys the
excitement of a racing track
while the arches suggest a
sense of control, reflecting the
handling power of the MINI.

! For this project, the student chose to
design an exhibition stand for the launch
of two new concept cars in celebration of
MINI's fiftieth birthday: the MINI Coupé
and the MINI Roadster.

At the concept model stage two possible
concepts emerged; one using the idea of
a 'ribbon' of racetrack through the stand,
the other a series of arches evocative of
'matchbox' cars. In the final design, a
combination of these three-dimensional
elements was used. Both initial sketch
ideas were expressed in the final
computer-generated client visuals. The
stand also offers an exclusive giveaway
in the form of an 'Airfix' coupé 'kit',
allowing visitors to build their own scaled
model of the car. This idea is echoed on
the stand at full size, adding a sense of
playfulness to the brand message.

The final design effectively combines the
cheeky MINI spirit and the racing pedigree
of the MINI Coupé.

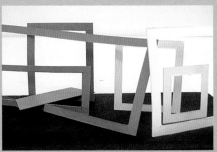

= A concept model of
the arch elements.

= A concept model of the
ribbon racetrack element.

= Computer-generated visual
showing the final overall design
for the stand.

? Imagine you have been asked to design a single-storey exhibition stand
for a well-known mobile phone company at a major trade show in America.
The space will be a 6 x 8 m (19 x 26 ft) peninsular site, open on three sides with
a 4 m-high wall along one of the 8 m (26 ft) sides. Elements can be hung from
the venue roof, but must not be more than 4 m (13 ft) high from the ground.

1   Your client requires a welcome area, a small bar and seating area for
    hospitality, an area for an interactive display and a more private area with
    Internet access for private discussion. How can you effectively design
    for the needs of your client in such a small space?

2   Using the idea of 'mobile communication for an international business
    market', explore possible spatial ideas through a series of two-dimensional
    sketching and three-dimensional modelling. Can you identify the strongest
    of your ideas?

3   How will your preferred concept support the client's message?
    Where will you apply the company logo to best effect?

4   How will visitors to the stand use the space? Is it possible for some area to
    be multi-functional? How will the exhibition 'stand out' from the competition?

Our relationship with space is not neutral: spaces evoke emotional responses.

For the exhibition designer, the implication of this is that each design decision brings with it subliminal narratives, which communicate to visitors. Whether this is through form, space, surface, materiality, light or sound, the space will develop an atmosphere that evokes feeling.

Some exhibition spaces may offer the visitor a passive experience, where information is delivered predominantly through images, text and objects. In contrast, exhibitions designed to be interactive will immerse the visitor in a different kind of experience, where they may take on the role of 'performer' as well as audience.

Through developing an understanding of the relationship between the visitor and their surroundings, the exhibition designer has the opportunity to manipulate the nature of spaces in order to support the narrative.

Exhibition media Theatrical techniques

A theatrical approach to exhibition design divides up the space to create a series of 'sets' through which and within which the audience can move. Changes in height, scale, colour, sound, texture, surface and lighting all affect the atmosphere and character of the space, communicating particular spatial messages that act as a subliminal backdrop to the narrative.

= **GOODBYE & HELLO: DIALOGUE WITH THE BEYOND, MUSEUM OF COMMUNICATION** Bern, Switzerland

DESIGNER
= **GEWERK DESIGN**

DATE
= **2008**

This exhibition explored the idea of 'afterlife experiences'. The space, lined with black and white stripes, generated false perspectives and spatial illusions aimed at disturbing the visitor's perception and orientation. Accented with red pillars, the design successfully created an unknown and foreign environment to evoke 'the hereafter'.

Setting the scene

Whether they are designed for a cultural or commercial exhibition, the spatial arrangements and positioning of exhibition content will influence how visitors move through space, picking up messages and information along the way.

The spaces may host a variety of exhibition media, which may include audio-visual areas, interactive exhibits, objects on display and graphic communication. False perspective, or mirrors, can create the illusion of increased or decreased size, which is a well-recognised theatrical technique.

Theatrical gauzes can be used to 'reveal' information or ideas to surprise the visitor. A gauze stretched across a space will hide what is behind when lit from the front. The object, theatrical display or model is 'revealed' when the light on the gauze is removed and the display behind is lit.

A liquid-crystal film sandwiched between a polarised filter and glass sheets is opaque, providing privacy or a surface to receive projection. However, when an electric current is passed through the film, the crystals become aligned with the polarised filter, allowing light to pass through.

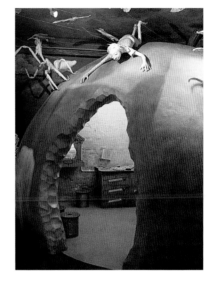

= **JAMES AND THE GIANT PEACH, ROALD DAHL CHILDREN'S GALLERY** Aylesbury, UK

DESIGNER
= **BREMNER AND ORR**

DATE
= **1996**

Themed environments or reconstructions, populated with mannequins or dressed with props, create displays popular with and easily understood by the public. Here, a giant 'peach' is used as a vehicle to tell a story about insects. The interior space has the scale of a playhouse where children can hunt out information about creepy crawlies. Every component of the area is themed around the story.

Exhibition media Theatrical techniques

= **SOVEREIGN HILL**
Ballarat, Australia

DESIGNER
= **SOVEREIGN HILL MUSEUMS**
ASSOCIATION

DATE
= **1970**

Human facilitators or demonstrators help
an audience to directly engage with exhibits
and ideas. Similarly, 'live actors', particularly
popular in heritage interpretation, can bring an
environment to life. Sovereign Hill in Ballarat,
Australia, is a reconstruction of an 1850s gold
mining town. The experience is populated
with actors playing the part of carefully
researched historical characters, who
interact with the public.

Performance

Actors and demonstrators, whether live or digital, are useful storytelling vehicles that can be successfully employed in exhibitions to add additional layers to the narrative.

The inclusion of mannequins 'in the white', or in full colour, gives audiences an immediate human connection to a story and a better understanding of the exhibit's scale. A 'talking head', created by projecting the filmed image of an actor onto a white moulded face, creates the illusion of live performance. Similarly, multiple 'talking heads' on flat-screen monitors can be positioned within an exhibit so that they appear to hold conversations with each other.

Holograms are a sophisticated form of projection that create the illusion of three-dimensional objects. High-definition 3D holograms can be projected through a specialised video system, generating life-size images into a live setting. Whilst virtual, the 'human' holograms interact in real time. For exhibition design this technology presents exciting opportunities for interpretive performance.

Storyboarding

Most commonly used in theatre and film, the storyboard is a technique for choreographing action through space and time. Storyboards usually take the form of a series of hand-drawn or computer-generated drawings, presented in sequence and showing selected moments of a progressing narrative. In exhibitions, the storyboard is employed for a range of different scenarios. In its simplest form it may illustrate graphically how something works, for example how electricity is generated in a power station. In this sense the storyboard acts as a method of interpretation. For a product launch at a trade fair, for example, the storyboard will indicate how performance space on the stand will change according to lighting, sound and special effects. Part working document, and part presentation piece, the storyboard acts as an effective way of communicating a very specific type of narrative as it changes in time.

? **'SUSPENSION OF DISBELIEF'**
This is a phrase used in theatre to describe the one basic requirement of an audience: they are asked to believe a performance is 'real' even though they know they are looking at a stage or screen. How might this idea be applied to themed exhibitions?

Exhibition media Theatrical techniques

Lighting the set

Lighting design is an art and discipline used to great effect in exhibitions. Light can be used to 'paint' an environment by adding colour, modelling and accent to the space and its objects, transforming its mood and atmosphere. Light can add a personality that differentiates connecting spaces, helping to lead visitors along a route through the exhibition.

The relationship between light and materials is often exploited in exhibitions. Translucent materials can be backlit, creating walls of glowing light, whilst fibre optic lights set into a black surface create the illusion of a starry sky. Coloured filters and theatrical gels offer creative possibilities when used with up-lighters and down-lighters. Surfaces may be washed, or simply edged with light.

The juxtaposition of red, green and blue light can create almost any colour combination. Light Emitting Diodes (LEDs) are special chips that emit light when electricity is applied. They can be programmed to change colour over time. Energy efficient and long lasting, LEDs can be used as single bulbs to create a range of different colour combinations or can be used together for large screen displays.

A white surface will reflect the colour of the light that falls upon it, but an already coloured surface will have more complicated results. Interesting research has taken place into how the original colour painted onto the front of cathedrals, now lost through time and weathering, can be evoked using projection.

: **EDOUARD MANET**
The most important person in a picture is light.

? **'PEPPER'S GHOST'**
'Pepper's Ghost' is a technique for showing change. It originates from the smoke and mirror techniques of the theatre, originally used to create the illusion of 'Banquo's ghost' in *Macbeth*. It involves an angled sheet of glass, which reflects images, some of which may be hidden from the viewer. In recent years the technique has been used in many different ways and designers revel in finding new ones.

= **SWEDISH PAVILION, WORLD EXPO 2008**
Zaragoza, Spain

DATE
= **1970**

In Sweden's expo pavilion, the verticality of the tree trunks suggests a Swedish forest, whilst a gobo projected onto the floor evokes dappled light coming through the tree canopy. A 'gobo' is a theatrical lighting device that can create the illusion of light falling through a venetian blind, or water flowing under a bridge. They can be custom made into signs or logos, and the addition of coloured gels and a motor to rotate them can help to create movement and mood.

Exhibition media Cinematic techniques

Multimedia exhibitions will frequently use technology to deliver both cultural and commercial messages. Choosing the most appropriate media for communication is a priority for the exhibition designer. Audio-visual displays and the use of projection provide useful and flexible opportunities for storytelling. Audio-visual is often the media of choice for introductory areas, firmly positioning an audience in the story.

MISHA BLACK
We have entered the realm where the designer may assume the cloak of the advertising man, the film director or the professional illusionist, while he decides the best way of conveying his message to the unsuspecting visitor in a whisper, or shout, as the occasion may require.

Projection

Effective front or back projection requires low lighting levels. Ideally, audio-visual presentations would take place in a controlled space that is ergonomically designed according to the size of audience, the timing of the show and the requirements of the projection. Suppliers can give examples of light throw for front projection, although it should be remembered that shadows will be cast if the audience walks in front of the screen. Back projection avoids this problem, although space needs to be allocated behind the screen to accommodate projection paraphernalia. Back projection can be much brighter because it is transmitted rather than reflected light.

Practical design considerations include seating, audience sight-lines, control of sound, control of ambient light, entrances and exits that do not interfere with the visitor experience, trigger controls at the entrance, and an alternative exhibition route for visitors who wish to avoid the audio-visual. Presentations should be short, most commonly less than three minutes – any longer and visitors' attention may be lost.

Alternatively, high-definition (HD) plasma screens may be used singly or as 'video walls', and can be configured in both portrait and landscape format. For architecturally scaled screens, LED bulbs work together to produce huge, seamless images when viewed from a distance, for example at a football match or concert.

= **360° PROJECTION
AND LASERS**

DESIGNER
= **VERTIGO SYSTEMS**

Projection and laser displays can create spectacular effects for the exhibition designer.

Exhibition media Cinematic techniques

= **THE SOUNDGARDEN AT EUREKA! THE NATIONAL CHILDREN'S MUSEUM**
Halifax, UK

DESIGNER
= **NORTHERN LIGHT CODESIGN**

The 'SoundGarden' is an immersive gallery dedicated for under-fives. The scale, level of interactivity, subject matter and use of colour have been designed to engage its young audience.

= **TALKING BOX IN THE LANDSCAPE**

DESIGNER
= **ATS HERITAGE**

Talking boxes can be run by solar electricity when used outside and respond when buttons are pressed, enabling interesting opportunities for interpretation in the landscape.

Sound

The use of audio, from music and sound effects to the spoken voice, is an additional sensory dimension for visitors to an exhibition environment. The echoing sound of dripping water will make a recreated dungeon feel cold and wet, whilst the sound of seagulls and laughter is reminiscent of a day at the seaside. Like light, ambient sound effects and soundscapes evoke atmosphere and feeling that enhance the narrative.
A conversation overheard in a historic house from a door ajar to the kitchens, supported by the banging of pots and the smells of cooking, helps us to imagine what the kitchen was like, even if it can't be seen. Light beam 'triggers' that set off sound effects when broken by a visitor save energy and the nerves of attendants.

? **EXHIBITION TECHNOLOGIES**
Exhibition technologies impact on the environment. Twenty audio tours have been commissioned for a historic site. What consideration should be given to their 'life-cycle of energy' in terms of their use and eventual disposal?

The sophistication of satellite navigation or global positioning systems (GPS) technology offers wayfinding and interpretation opportunities that enable the visitor to break out of the exhibition space. This image illustrates how the combination of technology and the use of an actor can help to bring a historic environment to life.

The management of sound in busy immersive environments is a significant challenge for the exhibition designer. Sound spill from one area of an exhibition to another is at best irritating and at worst confusing for the visitor. The position of non-reflective, sound absorbing surfaces or directional 'sound showers', are useful in confining sound within relevant areas. Alternatively sound may be controlled by delivery through individual hand-held devices or sound posts. Oral history projects that have collected sound as a historical archive may be delivered in a themed object, for example a period radio or telephone, depending on the design narrative.

Induction loops enable those with hearing aids to have a similar experience to hearing visitors; however, spoken audio tours should also be provided as printed material.

Mobile technologies

Portable digital information systems, including mobile phones, have extended the exhibition designer's communication pallet. Through the use of actors, music and sound effects, audio tours can add extra layers of information to an exhibition, where other forms of interpretation may be problematic or distracting. This may be the case in art galleries, or culturally sensitive environments, such as religious sites.

Audio tours can also be dedicated to meet the needs of specific audiences, for example blind or partially sighted visitors, tours specifically adapted for children or, in contrast, subject specialists. Audio brings useful additional layers of interpretation and subject detail that the listener can control or return to.

Exhibition media Interactivity

INTERACTIVE PLAY

Puzzles, feely boxes, dressing up,
lift-up flaps, rubbings and stamps are
typical of 'low tech' interactive exhibits.
These types of interactive element are
relatively easy to manufacture, maintain
and explain to audiences.

Interactive exhibits provide a valuable mechanism for explaining a range of often difficult information. The act of physically and intellectually engaging with an exhibit, rather than passively receiving information, creates an interaction between the exhibit and audience that aims to facilitate learning.

Interactive exhibits

The element of learning though 'play' evoked by interactive games and puzzles is particularly, although not exclusively, enjoyed by children. As with games and toy design, the exhibition designer needs to be clear about the purpose of the interactive. How do the players 'win' or in the case of an interactive, 'get the message'? The best games can be understood very quickly, with only a short explanation. Instructions therefore need to be kept to a minimum and the interactive easy to operate and reset. If the interactive does not communicate quickly, the visitor will give up and move to another part of the exhibition.

Interactive exhibits create wonderful moments, when the engagement with an exhibition changes to a more immersive experience, hopefully followed by a 'eureka' moment for the visitor, when they understand the message or succeed in a task.

Interactivity is particularly popular in children's museums because it helps to create lively learning environments. However, the whole environment needs to consider the needs of this particular visitor: heights, graphics and a range of communication will require input from educational specialists. Will the exhibition support a whole class of school children? Is there an education centre? Is there somewhere to eat a packed lunch?

Exhibition media Interactivity

= **NOSY PARKER, BALANCE
AND POWER EXHIBITION,
KRANNERT ART MUSEUM
Illinois, USA**

DESIGNER
= **ANTENNA DESIGN**

DATE
= **2005**

The stools in this exhibition appear to be
gallery furniture, but once visitors sit down,
a camera that is looking up starts taking
pictures of the visitor. The images are then
projected down onto the floor and float
between the stools, evoking an exchange.

Digital interactives

As new digital technologies are developed, they offer interesting opportunities for designing interactive environments. These areas of development run in parallel with the growing influence of digital art installations, where technologies are used as new tools for artists wishing to explore ways of creating 'live' interactive 'moments' created by the behaviour of the visitor. Some of these works exist in a state of constant change and evolution.

Digital interactives are usually made up of a wide range of technologies that interact with each other. These include digital sensors, cameras, tracking and the feedback of digital information. For example, a seemingly ordinary surface may receive projection from overhead, but when the viewer touches the image, the movement is picked up by a camera which feeds back information to a computer, triggering a response in the projection.

Touch-screen computers have become a familiar part of our everyday lives. Development of multi-touch-screen computers offers exciting opportunities for group participation between visitors, making a potentially more enjoyable experience for families, as well as creating interesting interactions between strangers. Plasma screens no longer need to be static. Sliding and even rotating plasma screens that show synchronised films create interesting 'attracts' in commercial exhibitions, whilst also delivering important messages.

= **MULTI-TOUCH-SCREEN COMPUTERS**

DESIGNER
= **VERTIGO SYSTEMS**

Multi-touch-screen computers offer exciting opportunities for interaction between visitors. Instead of a solitary experience, this technology adds an additional social dimension to digital play.

: CHARLES EAMES
In doing an exhibition... one deliberately tries to let the fun out of the bag. The catch is it can't be any old fun but it must be a very specialised brand. The excitement, or joke, must be a working part of the idea. The fun must follow all the rules of the concept involved.

Exhibition media Display

= **MEDIEVAL AND RENAISSANCE GALLERIES, VICTORIA & ALBERT MUSEUM**
London, UK

Glass cabinets can be 'bespoke', which means they are specifically manufactured for a project, or can be bought ready made. In terms of visitor experience, the most successful glass cabinet displays allow the visitor to engage with 'the authentic object', taking care not to create physical and psychological barriers for visitors.

Of course, one of the main considerations for the exhibition designer, whether working commercially or culturally, is how the objects or products will be displayed. This is an important part of exhibition design: for many visitors, the items on display are the main reason for attending the exhibition.

Display units

Glass cabinets play a significant role in the display of valuable or vulnerable objects, particularly in museum environments. When objects are delicate in terms of conservation, they will require the security and protection of a display case in order to control access, humidity, lighting and temperature as necessary. Similarly, close collaboration is required with the curator and conservation specialists to ensure that objects chosen as part of a specific narrative are compatible in terms of conservation.

The height of cases and objects needs to be suitable for all visitors, whilst still creating interesting and beautiful displays. The use of platforms and acrylic boxes to create different levels within a case is useful as are a host of invisible fixings used to safely secure precious or delicate objects.

Thought should be given to supporting backgrounds in cases. What colours and types of surface will most appropriately support the objects? Bright colours that detract from the display are best avoided, although the contrast of neutral tones between object and background can help objects stand out. For very small objects, accompanying large-scale images or magnifications are helpful to visitors.

Lighting can transform a display, helping to model objects and create light and shade. 'Accent' or spot lighting an object immediately highlights it as something of significance. When there are issues of conservation, low-level halogen lighting may be used. Whilst useful for displaying transparent objects, such as glass, care should be taken to avoid light boxes that turn an object into a silhouette.

Exhibition media Display

= **FIBRE OPTIC LIGHTING**

Fibre optic lighting consists of
long flexible fibre optic 'tails',
which carry light directly to
where it is needed. The lamp
housing, where a great deal
of heat is generated, can be
placed remotely or safely
outside the case. Here the fibre
optic light is used to light part
of a white card model.

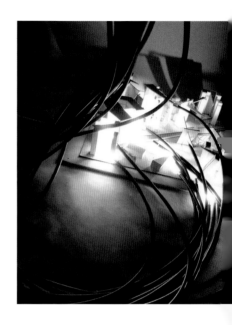

Exhibition models

The universal accessibility of models
makes them valuable communicative
tools. They help to illustrate an overall
understanding of spatial relationships,
acting as three-dimensional maps that
help us to navigate our way through a
narrative. Models of reconstructions
help us to imagine sites that no longer
exist. A model illustrating the layout of a
Roman fort, for example, enables us to
see how the fort was laid out, its main
thoroughfares and the relationships
between significant buildings, helping
us to gain a better understanding of
how people lived and worked. Often
models 'in the white' help to emphasise
a particular part of a story without the
distraction of colour. For example, a
white model in the Holocaust Gallery
of London's Imperial War Museum
showing passengers from one train
arriving at Auschwitz, very effectively
illustrates the scale of this horror.

Comparative models are useful in
demonstrating layers of history or
changes through time, used most
successfully as a 'Pepper's Ghost'
(see page 92). Maquette is another
name for scaled industrial or prototype
models that offer useful commercial
display opportunities. Full-size model
prototypes may be completely empty
of mechanism, but when the way an
object 'looks' is the main thrust of its
marketing, the model is very useful.
On occasion, models may be working
mechanisms, or automata used to
illustrate a process or physical principle

= **MODEL OF BEIJING, BEIJING URBAN PLANNING CENTRE**
Beijing, China

This shows just part of a huge model of the city of Beijing in China. The World Trade Centre site is in the foreground looking west down Jianuomenwai, towards the Palace Museum. On display is a vast modern city, confidently about to host the 2008 Olympic Games.

? **ACCESS**
Do you enjoy a varied diet? Fish and chips or sushi? Burger or roast beef? Popcorn or apple pie? What is your taste in exhibitions? Do you think broadening access is something to enjoy? Is 'dumbing down' a recipe for disaster? Should we be selective in our cultural diets?

Exhibition media Display

? **REAL OBJECTS**
People enjoy engaging with 'real' objects.
At the Osaka Expo in 1970, both the USSR
and the USA had spectacular pavilions, full
of space technology. However, there was
one significant difference that gave the
American experience the edge; moon rock.

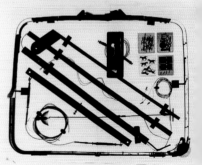

= **TOURISMS: SUITCASE STUDIES,**
WALKER ART CENTER
Minneapolis, USA

DESIGNER
= **DILLER, SCOFIDIO + RENFRO**

DATE
= **1991**

In their design for a travelling exhibition,
'Tourisms', Diller, Scofidio + Renfro used
50 suitcases to represent each of the US
states. Each case contained a description
and a commentary on a famous landmark
within that state, and was hung from a
ceiling-mounted rod. The design of the
display cases meant that the exhibition was
flexible and easy to move to other locations.

Exhibition media Student case study

PROJECT
= 'ENERGISE' AT EUREKA!

DESIGNER
= AMANDA PHILLIPS

DATE
= 2007

= Concept drawing
showing the
'Energize Point'.

! This project was based at the National
Children's Museum 'Eureka!' in Halifax,
UK. It was an educational exhibition aime
at teaching young children about
sustainability and environmental issues,
using the home as a vehicle for the story
The exhibition was scaled and designed
to appeal to a young audience, engaging
them in 'islands of interpretation' where
interactives would help them to learn
about green issues. Design consideratic
was given to a range of sustainable
materials in support of the exhibition.
Children move around the space explor
the kitchen, living room and bathroom
exhibits before moving outside on to the
roof terrace. Children carry with them a
'Energize Stick' in the form of a low-ene
light bulb, and through games and quiz
they can charge up the bulb at various
points. A 'Big Feet' interactive also help
children to gain an understanding of the
concept of a 'Carbon Footprint', with a
memory foam floor covering!

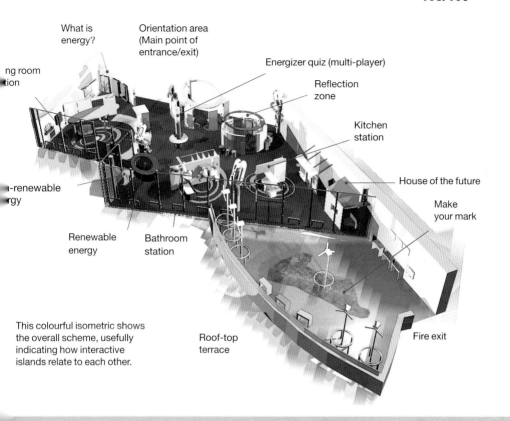

What is
energy?

Orientation area
(Main point of
entrance/exit)

Energizer quiz (multi-player)

ng room
tion

Reflection
zone

Kitchen
station

-renewable
gy

House of the future

Make
your mark

Renewable
energy

Bathroom
station

This colourful isometric shows
the overall scheme, usefully
indicating how interactive
islands relate to each other.

Roof-top
terrace

Fire exit

Imagine you have been asked to design an exhibition
called 'The Viking Family' in a 10 x 15 m (32 x 49 ft) museum
gallery with a ceiling height of 3.4 m (11 ft). The gallery will
house a collection of recently discovered domestic objects
from a Viking site, including cooking and storage pots,
parts of domestic furniture, leather clothing and shoes
and a box thought to contain traces of medicinal herbs.

What exhibition media could be used to support the
story of Viking domestic life? How can 'real' objects
be used to support the story?

How could you interpret how the artefacts might
have been made? How would they have been used
and by whom?

How will you introduce an element of interactivity into
the exhibition that will appeal to a younger audience?

Are there any scenarios where you think certain types
of media may be inappropriate in this particular
exhibition? Can you justify your decisions?

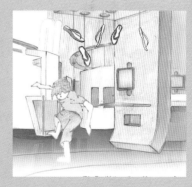

= Concept drawing showing
the 'Big Feet' interactive.

Graphic design involves bringing type and image together to communicate a message, and in this sense, it can play an important role in the formation of the exhibition 'script'. It provides the foundations of the interpretive bridge between the expert curator or brand manager and the public.

In an exhibition, the design of the graphics and three-dimensional components should be inextricably linked. It is tempting to separate out graphics as a discipline, but exhibition designers do this at their peril. In the most successful projects, exhibition designers, graphic designers and copywriters work together to create a consistent design language that pulls the story together in a logical narrative, with a clear rhythm and consistency.

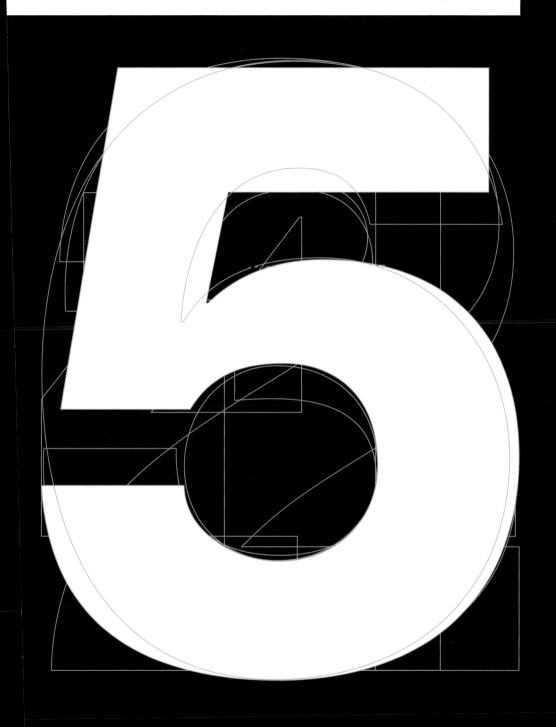

Exhibition graphics Typography

Throughout the exhibition, text will be used to help communicate the story to the visitor. It is vital that the exhibition designer has a good knowledge of typography and how best to communicate to all audiences.

Typefaces

There are thousands of typefaces to choose from and these can be classified by a number of systems. Here, they are divided into seven groups based on their historical development, and changes brought about by the digital revolution:

Humanist

Old Style

Transitional

Modern

Slab serif

Sans serif

Postmoder

= **PROJECT MAH JONGG,
MUSEUM OF JEWISH HERITAGE**
New York, USA

DESIGNER
= **PENTAGRAM**

DATE
= **2010**

A carefully selected typeface will help
to communicate the story to a visitor.
For this exhibition, which tells the story
of Mah Jongg, an ancient Chinese
tile-based game, the designers selected
Fregio Mecano, a 1920s Machine Age
face that resembles joined tiles.

Legibility and readability

Legibility concerns the relative clarity of letterforms, both individually and when set together to form words. Readability is about how easily the text is understood, for example its point size, line length and spacing between lines of text. The following guidelines are useful basic starting points in understanding the important subtleties to be considered when dealing with type.

TYPEFACE
The larger the 'x' height, the larger text appears on the page. Space between letters is adjusted by 'tracking'. Avoid 'fashionable' fonts for permanent exhibitions; they may quickly date. The use of upper- and lower-case letters gives more information to the shape of words, making them easier to read, particularly at a distance.

SCALE
The size of letterforms is controlled by point size. The required point size is dependent on the viewing distance of the audience and available lighting. Sans serif fonts appear to be more legible at a distance. The minimum type size for body text should be 18-36 points. However, creating mock-ups to be used at actual size is a useful mechanism for making judgements on site.

'X' height
Height of the lower-case 'x' in a designed typeface - varies from typeface to typeface. The 'x' height (with no ascender or descender) represents the 'mass' or 'body' of the typeface.

LINES OF TEXT

On average, line lengths of 66 characters (approximately 10 words) enable the reader to comfortably scan back to the start of the next line. When lines of text are placed too close together vertically, the letterforms appear to run into each other. When lines are too far apart, text loses its identity as a graphic element.

COLOUR

There should be a tonal contrast of at least 70 per cent between type and background. Dark type on a light background offers good legibility. Although black type on white is the most legible, white on black is not very restful to read at length. Yellow should never be used for type and avoid using busy underlying images that distract from important messages.

LIGHTING

Lighting is essential for good legibility. When projecting or backlighting text avoid letterforms with relatively thin components. Projection surfaces need to be flat and smooth to avoid distortion. Matt surfaces should be used.

? **RELATIVES**
A font is a set of characters of one size of typeface. It will include capitals, lower-case small capitals, figures, fractions, ligatures, mathematical signs, punctuation and reference marks.

Exhibition graphics   Graphic families

= **CHURCHILL MUSEUM
CHURCHILL WAR ROOMS,**
London, UK

DESIGNER
= **CASSON MANN**

GRAPHIC DESIGN
= **NICK BELL DESIGN**

DATE
= **2005**

Three typefaces were used in the design of the Churchill Museum.
They were not chosen to signal differences in information hierarchy
but were used to give personality to the voices in the interpretation
and create differentiation between them.

Datum lines on the grey 'story' and 'sub-story' panels meant that
all voices appeared in consistently the same place on the panel
so visitors get used to knowing where to look for particular types
of information. The size and verticality of the panels effectively
isolates the interpretation text, making it more comfortably
readable against a busy backdrop of museum objects, structures
and textures. Story titles were singled out by being set vertically
and emphasised through illumination.

The use of a consistent graphics structure throughout an exhibition helps to link areas and stories, offering visitors a logical visual anchor. It is the layout and structure, rather than the use of colour or imagery, which enable us to recognise these similarities.

Harmony and contrast

Finding a consistent graphic structure starts with a choice of two or three typefaces. Some work better together than others, but an ideal is to create clear contrasts. Serif and sans serif typefaces are an obvious example. The weight, shape, size and width of the letterforms will create word shapes with internal patterns that will have a particular visual structure. This will carry expressive qualities that resonate with each other. When this works successfully, exhibition messages are clarified or enhanced.

These distinctive characteristics should influence the choices of typeface according to the nature of the story and its audience. The main title typeface may be a more stylised type, whereas the body text must focus on legibility. If required, a third typeface may be chosen for image labelling as a subtle variation from the body text.

A family feel to the graphics comes by making basic design decisions that are consistent throughout the exhibition, such as the type size, proportion, spacing and line length. Also, the layout of information and the use of bands of pattern, graphic motifs or logos may also prove helpful. Once a clear structure is established, subtle changes in design may include the use of colour and imagery. Change may take place in different areas or themes without losing a logical sense of continuity.

The sophistication of graphic production has given the designer far greater freedom to experiment with combinations of text and images. To an extent this has liberated designers from the use of the traditional rectangular graphic 'panel'. However, the approach above still applies, and in many circumstances the graphic panel remains a useful exhibition tool.

Exhibition graphics   Graphic families

Hierarchies of information

The use of graphic grids to organise the layout of images and text supports the vertical, horizontal and diagonal structure of typefaces. The layering of information into three or four levels of information within the grid helps visitors quickly decide how much they wish to read. Text should be kept to a minimum and for a graphic panel an accepted norm is to avoid using more than 150 words.

: JAMES GARDNER

Fortunately exhibitions can do some things that books can never do, principally by providing an occasion in which the public can actively participate. It is much more fruitful to treat exhibitions like this rather than as explanatory leaflets that cannot be taken home.

= **HIERARCHIES OF INFORMATION**

MAIN TITLE
= This forms the header for a section and is the first level of information. This needs to make a visual as well as a literal 'statement'.

SUB TITLE
= This should be a short summary of the key points of the story and acts in the same way as the bold paragraph at the start of a newspaper article.

BODY TEXT
= This forms the main body of the text and carries more detailed information. The body text needs to be laid out in short paragraphs, punctuated with images or examples. Text can be ranged left (which is easier to read) or right. Justified text sits in a block with straight edges. Paragraphs should be no more than two or three short sentences, with a space before the next. Take care when greatly enlarging justified text as the spaces between words become exaggerated.

IMAGE TITLE
= This is the short caption that accompanies and explains images.

Main title

5

Sub title

Lorem ipsum dolor sit amet, consectetur adipisicing elit, sed do eiusmod tempor incididunt ut labore et dolore magna aliqua.

Ut enim ad minim veniam, quis nostrud exercitation ullamco laboris nisi ut aliquip ex ea commodo consequat. Duis aute irure dolor in reprehenderit in voluptate velit esse cillum dolore eu fugiat nulla pariatur.

Excepteur sint occaecat cupidatat non proident, sunt in culpa qui officia deserunt mollit anim id est laborum.

Lorem ipsum dolor sit amet, consectetur adipisicing elit, sed do eiusmod tempor incididunt ut labore et dolore magna aliqua.Excepteur sint occaecat cupidatat non proident, sunt in culpa qui officia deserunt mollit anim id est laborum.

GP02

Image title

Lorem ipsum dolor sit amet, consectetur adipisicing elit, sed do eiusmod tempor incididunt ut labore et dolore magna aliqua.

GP01

Lorem ipsum dolor sit amet, consectetur adipisicing elit, sed do eiusmod tempor incididunt ut labore et dolore magna aliqua.

Ut enim ad minim veniam, quis nostrud exercitation ullamco laboris nisi ut aliquip ex ea commodo consequat. Duis aute irure dolor in reprehenderit in voluptate velit esse cillum dolore eu fugiat nulla pariatur.

Excepteur sint occaecat cupidatat non proident, sunt in culpa qui officia deserunt mollit anim id est laborum.

Image Title

GP03

Image Title

GP04

LOGO

Exhibition graphics Graphic families

Understanding

The nature of the exhibition audience determines the design approach to graphic communication. An expert copywriter should be employed to produce clear, unambiguous language.

Braille should be included for blind or partially sighted audiences, particularly when there is an opportunity for tactile engagement. Braille should always be placed consistently throughout an exhibition so that it can be easily found, and a printed label included nearby for escorts. When scripting for Braille (and audio) there may be subtle differences in wording to ensure that each is equally easy to understand.

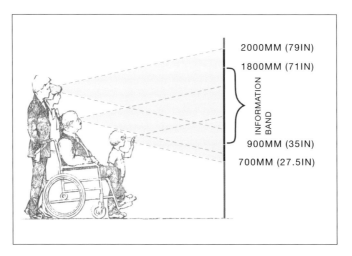

2000MM (79IN)

1800MM (71IN)

INFORMATION BAND

900MM (35IN)

700MM (27.5IN)

= INFORMATION BAND HEIGHTS

The design of exhibition graphics requires careful organisation so that important information remains at heights accessible to the majority of visitors.

= **INTERNATIONAL MESSAGES WORLD EXPO 2008**
Zaragoza, Spain

DESIGNER
= **ZAHA HADID**

DATE
= **2008**

At expo, the international nature of the audience means that messages need to be delivered very simply and in a range of languages. Ideally, messages should be delivered predominantly by images and text kept to a minimum.

Similarly, the use of graphics in children's exhibitions, including interactive and object labels, will need to consider literacy levels, child-friendly typefaces and content as well as engaging imagery.

Some specialist exhibitions, particularly in the commercial 'trade only' sector, may be aimed at very specialised audiences. The competitive pressures of commerce require exhibition graphics that offer clear, simple graphic sound bytes, a focus on clear branding and supporting imagery. More detailed information can be accessed through hard copy literature or digitally, via websites or touch-screen computers. Visual branding, through the use of the logo, imagery and text, has a powerful role in supporting the marketing messages of the stand and its success as a brand communicator.

Exhibition graphics   Graphic families

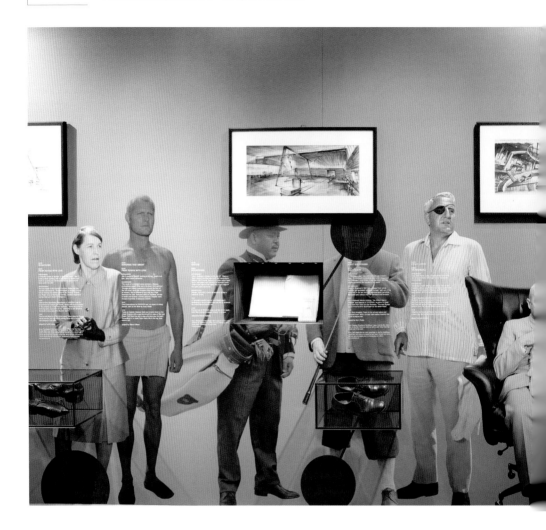

= **'FOR YOUR EYES ONLY'
JAMES BOND EXHIBITION,
IMPERIAL WAR MUSEUM**
London, UK

DESIGNER
= **CASSON MANN**

DATE
= **2008**

This image illustrates how the use
of graphic material can support
display. The use of a background
grid successfully helps images,
text and display to relate to each
other. The use of red adds an
accent of colour, drawing attention
to the cased objects.

Exhibition graphics   Graphics and communication

Developments in printing technologies have enabled graphics to be applied to a range of surfaces at large scale. This also offers opportunities for multi-purpose display. Spaces cut into the graphic can receive display cases for objects, interactive exhibits or plasma screens; objects displayed on the surface of the graphic and lighting can be embedded in the panel. The graphic information becomes an integral part of an exhibit, helping to bring a logic and clarity to the narrative.

Labelling

Labels, whether these are for instructions for interactive exhibits or for objects on display, need to be legible and easily understood. Whilst no one size fits all, it should be remembered that we have an aging population who appreciate the use of larger letters. Difficult or specialist language will exclude the majority of the public. Labelling objects in cases requires careful thought. Ideally, labels should be placed adjacent to objects. Where this is not possible alternative systems may be used, including numbering objects or graphic diagrams where objects are silhouetted but relate to a numbered list.

Graphics
A combination of words and images designed to convey a message.

= BOULLE MARQUETRY ,
CONSERVATION GALLERY
AT THE WALLACE COLLECTION
London, UK

This display case effectively tells the story of Boulle
Marquetry, an eighteenth-century French technique
for crafting decorative furniture. A graphic panel
takes up the back wall of the display case, and
samples of the materials used for this process
(types of wood veneer, mother of pearl and gold
leaf) are displayed alongside explanatory text.
At the base of the graphic a reconstruction of a
small box, placed on a dais, illustrates methods of
construction alongside original tools. As the dais
rotates, text on its surface explains the order of
the processes, as well as bringing movement and
interest to the display. To the right, a life-size, flat
graphic of a cabinet is an exemplar of a final object.
The case is lit to add modelling and drama to
the objects. The combination of text, diagram,
contemporary illustration, reconstruction, lighting
and actual artefact, effectively explains a difficult
story in an integrated and engaging way.

Exhibition graphics Graphics and communication

Interactive graphics

Sophisticated graphic production techniques and developments in digital technologies have paved the way for greater integration of interactivity with graphics.

Touch-screen computers have become a useful, alternative mechanism for the delivery of information, enabling the visitor to explore topics to a greater depth. However, there is a danger that this type of delivery of information contradicts the rationale of an exhibition. Would this level of detail be better provided elsewhere, by a supporting website or perhaps a book? Computers are of benefit when they help to clarify messages, through the use of animation, for example. They are an opportunity for a different type of graphic interactivity that should always be considered.

Exhibitions aimed at families are most popular when they offer the audience the opportunity to get involved with the stories of real people. By offering them the opportunity to take on the role of a real person, this character then becomes a vehicle within which particular stories can be told. For example, an exhibition about the *Titanic* may offer visitors a ticket with the description of a real character that boarded the fateful ship. What was their experience? Did they survive? Their 'ticket' becomes a way of personalising the experience for them, helping to identify with the passengers involved. Similarly a 'ticket' may become a mechanism by which visitors connect with the exhibition in other ways.

Exhibitions about controversial or current issues may use interactive graphics to engage their audience in 'feedback' of some kind. This type of participative interaction leads to additional updating of information, which not only gives visitors a sense of involvement, but is a useful technique for creating sustainable exhibitions. This may be a simple paper-based method or a more sophisticated digital mechanism that triggers action and reaction to the display.

= **THE DARWIN CENTRE,
NATURAL HISTORY MUSEUM**
London, UK

DESIGNER
= **AT LARGE**

DATE
= **2009**

The integration of touch-screen computers in this display case enable visitors to research the objects on display. If visitors wish to find out mo later, they can swipe the bar code on their entry ticket and this will enable them to return to a specific point in the centre's website at a later date.

Exhibition graphics Graphic production

= A SELECTION OF GRAPHIC SUBSTRATES

The way graphics are 'finished' depends on the
substrate used, the position of the graphics and
their use. Laser cutting technology has enabled
greater flexibility for the use of three-dimensional
type and sign making, enabling either the positive
or negative use of text.

When it comes to selecting materials for presenting graphic information, the choices are endless. The exhibition designer must draw on their knowledge to select the materials and production techniques that will best support the story behind their exhibition.

Graphics substrates

Graphic information can be ink-jet printed onto a wide range of different substrates, including paper, woven materials, medium-density fibreboard (MDF), plastics, recycled card and Foamex, which is a semi-rigid blown plastic. TYVEK is a printable plastic that looks like paper, but is fully recyclable. Materials also come in different thicknesses depending upon the design requirement, and 2 mm (0.08 in) Foamex is particularly useful, as it can bend into a curve. As printer technology develops, so too does the possible list of substrates that can directly receive images and text. Paper can be printed at large widths, of up to 6 m (19 ft).

Photographic quality printing can be produced using either the Cibachrome or Lambda process, enabling photo-quality paper printing up to 1200 mm (47 in) in width to lengths of up to 30 m (98 ft). This enables graphics to be produced almost like wallpaper, and hung either vertically or horizontally.

Whilst important graphic information should not be put on the floor where it may be missed, the development of robust, laminated floor surfaces makes it possible to use graphics on the floor, as a decorative treatment or orientation method. Footprints, for example, may help visitors move around a space. Custom-weave carpet finishes are now available, made from 100 per cent polypropylene, which can be recycled.

The flexibility of woven materials lends itself to the creation of graphic banners and 'pop-up' exhibition graphics, which are portable and particularly useful for temporary promotional material. As information changes it is relatively easy to replace the graphic.

Self-adhesive vinyl comes in a wide variety of colours and finishes and can be laser cut to form decorative patterns as well as lettering. It is particularly useful for international, travelling exhibitions where vinyl graphics can be simply removed and replaced with another language. Vinyl is a cheap alternative to creating an etched glass effect. Similarly, 'dry transfer' or 'rubdown' techniques enable text to be printed on the reverse of a plastic film, which is then applied directly to a wall by a specialist contractor. This facilitates the use of smaller text which would be awkward to produce using laser-cut vinyl. Finally, text can be directly painted onto the wall, using low-impact paints that can be easily painted over when the exhibition changes.

Exhibition graphics Graphic production

= **EXHIBITION STAND GRAPHICS
FOR O.C. TANNER**
Chicago, USA

DESIGNER
= **MAUK DESIGN**

DATE
= **2008**

O.C. Tanner is an organisation that provides employee appreciation programmes for companies and corporations. This small but effective stand is like a three-dimensional 'graphic garden', where companies can 'grow their own people'. The stand is an excellent example of the aesthetic and communicative properties of graphic components in their own right.

Typography

The design of letterforms and their combination and arrangement
to communicate a message to best effect.

Exhibition graphics Navigation

Until visitors have a sense of place and direction, they are unable to engage with an experience. If they are distracted at this apparently superficial level, how can they then be expected to engage at a deeper level with more important information? Orientational signage is an essential design component for managing exhibition visitors, and is about a holistic understanding of their journey within a site.

Signage

Consider the needs of a visitor to a distillery for a particular brand of whisky, which includes a visit to the visitor centre and a tour around the distillery. How will the visitor find their way from the car park, to the visitor's centre entrance, to the reception desk, to the café, to the lavatories, to the exhibition gallery, to the meeting place for the tour, to the shop and finally back to the car park? The distillery is a busy working site with serious health and safety considerations. How will employees and visitors differentiate between workplace and tour signage?

All signage, whether directional or instructive, should be designed as an extension to the family of graphics used throughout the experience. Similarly, there needs to be a consistency between directional maps, leaflets and signage. It is helpful to adopt the typeface used for the body text of the exhibition and use colour, logos and symbols for support. Most importantly, signage and direction need to be clearly understood at a glance. Visitors also appreciate an indication of how long the experience will take, enabling them to plan their visit.

Signage should be simple, short and consistent. A good rule of thumb is to give signs that are 3 m (10ft) away, a letter height of between 100–170 mm (4 – 7 in), whilst smaller, more general signs should be about 70 mm (3 in) high.

Signage in the landscape can be both directional and interpretive. Where do I need to go and what am I looking at? For example, the skill of the archaeological artist is valuable in recreating how significant sites may have looked in the past. The use of portable digital GPS technologies provide interesting opportunities for wayfinding and interpretation (see page 97). Constructed trails, often supported with art or sculpture, can help move visitors around a site, as well as introducing an interactive element to the experience that may appeal in particular to younger audiences.

= **THE GREAT NORTH MUSEUM**
Newcastle, UK

GRAPHIC DESIGN
= **NICK BELL DESIGN**

DATE
= **2009**

An example of clear, well-designed and positioned signage, supporting the visitor experience. The design of the signage is consistently used throughout the exhibition.

? **PICTOGRAMS**
Like brand logos, pictograms are simple symbols or signs that communicate information quickly to an international audience. A theme park, for example, might show a simple image of a big wheel. Think about how you might design pictograms to indicate the following: palace, brand experience, expo?

Exhibition graphics Student case study

PROJECT
= **SINGAPORE PAVILION FOR
SHANGHAI EXPO 2010**

DESIGNER
= **JAMES DWYER**

DATE
= **2007**

! This imagined student brief was to design the Singapore Pavilion for the World Expo 2010 in Shanghai, China. In response to the theme 'Better City, Better Life', the pavilion for this project is entitled 'The City of Harmony'. The use of graphics is central to the narrative, leading visitors on a filmic journey over two levels. Through imagery visitors are given a taste of the unique contrasts and experiences found in Singapore. The graphics used focus on image rather than text, communicating easily to an international audience.

The design of the pavilion thus works to advertise the image and brand of Singapore to the rest to the world, encouraging guests to make it their next travel destination. The experience ends dramatically with a hydraulic 'Sky-bridge' – a combination of bridge and lift that transports visitors back to the ground floor through an exciting multimedia display of Singapore's space-age future.

? Imagine you have been asked to design a family of graphic information for a travelling natural history exhibition called 'Colourful Creatures: Animals of the Amazon Rainforest'. Each panel must include a selection of imagery but text must be kept to a minimum of 150 words. You do not need to write copy, but should indicate where text will be.

1 Using the idea of a hierarchy of information, how will you design five graphic panels of A1 size, with the following titles: Tree Dwellers, Creepy Crawlies, Rainforest Birds, Tropical Butterflies and Venomous Creatures?

2 How will the nature of the story influence the typeface you choose? Think about size and background colour contrasts.

3 Panels can be designed in landscape or portrait format. Whilst each panel will tell a different story, how can they be made to have a consistent design approach?

4 Design an introductory panel to the exhibition that is twice the size of the section panels. How can this be made to feel like it belongs to the same 'graphic family'?

= A rendered elevation
  of the space.

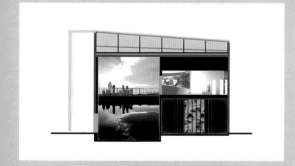

= Rendered elevations of
  the hydraulic 'Sky-bridge'.

The temporary nature of exhibitions means that they are large consumers of materials and energy. The environmental agenda is a significant ethical and design challenge at every stage of the design process.

The production and installation of an exhibition is also a complicated task. Multi-disciplinary in nature, exhibitions involve input from a variety of specialists who bring new voices to the project and present new strategic and organisational challenges.

Clear communication, including unambiguous technical drawing, is an essential practical and legal requirement in these final stages of the project. Whilst still a creative challenge for the designer, the focus now shifts to the practicalities of measuring, specifying and making.

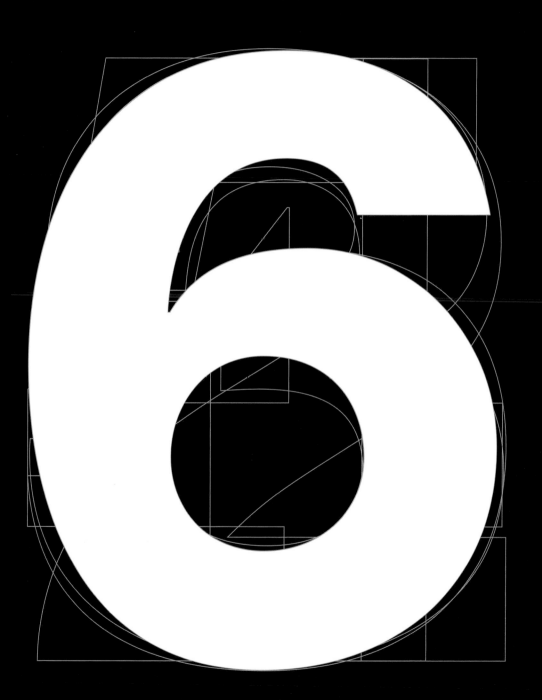

Putting on a show   Sustainability

Sustainability is a global concern and the responsibility of all participants in the exhibition design process. Whether it is the environmental strategies of large companies or museums, or the personal ethos of designers and their practice, environmental issues need to be addressed. These ideas go beyond the well recognised mantra of 'reduce, reuse and recycle'. Just as access issues have become a necessary legal and ethical requirement, sustainability is becoming embedded in all areas of working practice, from communication and interpretation, to social responsibility, and the cultural impact and influence of exhibitions. These ideas require ambitious ideals, but will be reinforced as new 'green' design chains become established.

Temporary design

The entire life-cycle of an exhibition – from the evaluation of the brief, its delivery and installation, to the end of its shelf life – will require an analysis of its environmental impacts. There may be some issues with compromise, but there will also be interesting problem-solving challenges requiring a holistic approach, and these should be relished by creative designers.

? **'EMBODIED ENERGY'**
This term describes the total energy required in extracting and then producing a material at a specified point. This calculation is complicated, but includes extraction, transportation, industrial manufacture, packaging and construction. Compare the embodied energy of the following simple tabletop interactive: a metal 'rubbing' of a panda; a coloured, wooden 'Panda' puzzle; a six-page plastic flip book.

= **CARDBOARD FIGURES, ASSOCIATION OF ISRAEL'S DECORATIVE ARTS (AIDA)**
Sculptural Objects & Functional Art (SOFA)

DESIGNER
= **Z-A STUDIO / GUY ZUCKER**

DATE
= **2008**

This award-winning, 'environmentally responsible' exhibition stand was commissioned by AIDA to display the work of four AIDA artists. The designers used large cardboard tubes, and cut them at 304 mm (12 in) increments to form lengths of 30–213 cm (1–7 ft). They then formed them into 'islands' of display for the artists. Platforms were laser cut from Plexiglas and lit from below by blue-hued, battery-powered discs of LED lights.

Putting on a show   Sustainability

Materials

Exhibitions have a tradition of experimenting with new materials and construction techniques. As more industries engage with a green agenda, the choice of sustainable materials also increases. Similarly, the development of laser cutting and digital fabrication technologies offers interesting and potentially less wasteful ways of creating new components for exhibitions.

Materials are chosen for their practical and aesthetic potential. When considered at the start of a project, they may become one of many inspirational triggers, and regular research for new materials can be invaluable. One of the skills of the designer is the ability to see alternative uses for materials and products. With imagination, even the humble colour swatch can be transformed into a tactile, colourful installation on a commercial exhibition stand.

The use of materials in the museum context often has to consider conservation requirements. In order to protect vulnerable collections, all materials and glues need to be lab-tested in advance of use. Colour choices in historical environments are more successful when they respect the historical development of colour, and its evocation of specific periods.

Sample material boards can provide valuable tactile information that are useful for decision making and appreciated by the client.

= **ASTELLAS MODULAR EXHIBIT KIT, EUROPEAN ASSOCIATION OF UROLOGY**
Stockholm, Sweden

DESIGNER
= **PHOTOSOUND**

DATE
= **2009**

Commercial exhibition design companies that take an ethical view of the life-cycle of exhibition stands often seek ways of designing spectacular bespoke modular components that can be reconfigured for different trade shows, thus extending the lifespan of the exhibition.

Specifications
Details of the dimensions, materials, methods of production, finishes and so on required to produce and install an exhibit or exhibition. In complex work they are also normally produced as a written document.

Putting on a show   Tendering

Once the design proposal for an exhibition has been approved by the client, the project is ready to start its transition from the workstation to the workshop.

PETER HIGGINS

The rarefied field of exhibition design provides a fascinating relationship between narrative storytelling, architectural space, the appropriate use of communication media, and an understanding of the visitor profile and business proposition. This is a complex blend of diverse disciplines that are normally taught independently, so anybody embarking on this roller coaster should be patient in gathering experience for what will ultimately be a rewarding profession that has a direct benefit for society.

The designer's role

The designer's role will now vary between projects. A 'turnkey' project simplifies the process for the client, making the designer responsible for the whole delivery of the exhibition, including quality and safety. By contrast, the separate appointment of the designer and contractors means that each takes responsibility for their own areas. For large-scale projects a project manager may be appointed who will work closely with the design team.

The process is further complicated when designing exhibitions for overseas venues. The designer and client have to navigate their way through a range of different trade practices, labour legislation, access to materials and skills as well as shipping arrangements. These potentially complicated issues can impact on the timescale and cost of delivery for the project.

The tendering process

The overall structure and quality of an exhibition is dependent upon the standards of workmanship of the main contractor. The tendering process involves inviting three or more recommended contractors to compete for 'tender'. The designer will send out identical packages of information that will need to be accurate and unambiguous. Any subsequent changes may accrue financial penalties later on. Mistakes are at best professionally embarrassing and at worst expensive or litigious.

Contractors need to be provided with the following basic information:

A covering letter about the project, including budget, timescale, details about the tendering process and the deadlines, contact details and a list of contents.

Exhibition rules, regulations and legal requirements, for example, ordinances about fire and health and safety.

General arrangement and detailed orthographic drawings.

Specifications: listing the materials, size, fixings, finishes, and colours.

Any other helpful visual information that will clarify the tender.

Specialist contractors

The main contractor may employ sub-contractors, such as electricians. However, multi-experiential exhibitions will potentially need a combination of specialist contractors, perhaps including some of the following:

THEATRICAL
Set fabricators, decorators, structural engineers, scenic contractors and artists, props and mannequin makers, flooring contractors and lighting specialists.

CINEMATIC
Multimedia specialists in film, video, audio, projection and laser.

INTERACTIVE
Interactive manufacturers, engineers and electronic experts and experts in digital technologies.

DISPLAY
Case manufacturers, environmental expertise, display lighting, artefact support and fixings, and model-makers.

GRAPHIC
Graphic designers, illustrators, printers, sign-makers and graphic panel fabricators.

Tendering package
A combination of different documents and drawings offered to potential contractors for the purpose of estimating costs or quoting a price. Tendering packages usually include an invitation to tender, general arrangement drawings, working drawings and detailed written specifications (including general clauses and conditions).

Putting on a show   Tendering

= **THE NATIONAL COLD WAR EXHIBITION, ROYAL AIR FORCE MUSEUM**
Cosford, UK

DESIGNER
= **NEAL POTTER**

DATE
= **2007**

This image is an excellent illustration of the challenges that designers and contractors have to face. Late in the design process an extra aircraft was added to the collection at the Royal Air Force Museum. Everyone seemed to think that the building was too full and the aircraft couldn't be included, but Potter looked at the task in a variety of dimensions and was able to take the unusual step of displaying the aircraft in a vertical suspension.

:   RICHARD MCCONNELL
Exhibitions happen in time as well as in space.

Technical communication

'Orthographic' or orthogonal drawing is a general design term used to describe technical communication in the form of scaled plans, elevations, sections, and detail drawings (see pages 74 – 75). At the concept stage of a project, plans and elevations are usually in sketch form but they will evolve as the design develops.

Technical drawings bring logic and sense to the design concept by using a range of universally understood conventions. They are a measure of the 'buildability' of design concepts. Final technical drawings are produced using Computer Aided Design (CAD) packages, facilitating a fast-track approach to technical communication and making it easier to work between individuals and teams.

Plans, elevations, sections and details form the main components of an orthographic drawing. A set of project drawings will start with the largest scale, usually 1:100, showing the context of the exhibition in the site. They then gradually focus in to show the overall exhibition, using interior scales of usually 1:50 and 1:20. Specific components are drawn using furniture scales of 1:10 or 1:5, and final details illustrating finishes and fixings will be drawn at 1:1 (actual size).

Ideally, details should be drawn on a separate sheet and cross referenced to the appropriate general arrangement sheets. Dimensions, annotations and symbols are like musical notation, providing useful shorthand for precise information when drawing. They need to be unambiguous and should answer the following basic questions about the exhibition and its built components:

Measurements: What size is it? Where is it? How much is needed?

Materials: What is it made from?

Methods of construction: How will it be built and function?

Finishes: How will it be finished?

Fixtures and fittings: Are there knobs, handles and light fittings?

The inclusion of human figures on the drawing at the development stage provides a useful sense of scale. However, they should be avoided in final technical drawings in order to avoid confusion with mannequins. Technical drawings can be very beautiful, and the careful use of line-weight can give them a three-dimensional quality as well as additional clarity. Elevations are often full of interesting structures and indications of where artefacts and graphics are to be positioned.

Putting on a show   Tendering

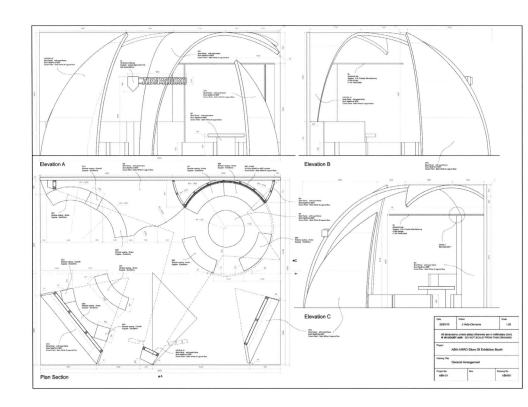

General Arrangement (GA) drawing

An orthographic drawing dimensioned to show the size and position of all significant elements, and annotated to identify each element and specify materials, methods of construction and finishes. All subsequent working drawings and detailed drawings are cross-referenced to the GA drawing. Normally an exhibition includes a GA plan showing the exhibit / exhibition site location.

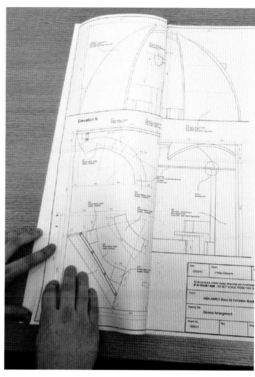

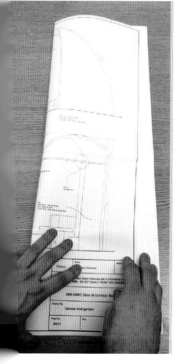

= FOLDING A GENERAL ARRANGEMENT DRAWING

In order to keep GA drawings safe and organised, they are usually folded for storage. This sequence of images shows how best to do this, so that the drawing can be easily located. In exhibition design, the general consensus is to place the plan in the bottom left-hand corner with an elevation or section shown directly above it and to the side, showing the close relationship between components. The information box and drawing number sit in the bottom right-hand corner, so that when folded this vital reference number is uppermost and can be easily found in a pile of drawings.

Putting on a show Building an exhibition

As with all interiors, the actual build is only a small part of the process. It is vital, however, that the exhibition designer remains involved in this stage, as they will need to ensure that the design concept, story and experience remain intact throughout.

Project management

The design, construction and installation of an exhibition are parts of a complicated process, requiring careful organisation and management. The role of the project manager is to oversee this process to ensure that each facet of the project runs on time, on budget and to a high quality.

A project planning matrix, plotting the time available for the project against the tasks required, enables everyone to see at a glance how areas will overlap and impact on each other. Certain tasks cannot start until others are finished, and everyone involved with the project is reliant on others to complete work to their specified deadlines if the project is to proceed smoothly.

All commercial exhibition organisers will have an exhibitors' manual, outlining the construction and health and safety rules and regulations that relate to each exhibition and with which all exhibitors are expected to comply contractually. This includes, for example, the national building regulations and the local rules relating to the venue. Part of the project manager's role is to oversee these processes.

Often, potentially costly problems in the final stages of the project are due to a lack of planning by the design team at the start. The project manager has a valuable organisational role that can help avoid these problems and he or she is an important communication conduit between the client, designer and contractors.

Health and safety

Early on in the exhibition design process a risk analysis of the project needs to be carried out in order to anticipate health and safety issues that need to be addressed.

For most large-scale exhibitions, the rules and regulations of a building site need to apply. In order to remain safe, all workers and visitors need to wear hard hats and boots and need to have received safety training.

= **THE MINE EXPERIENCE, BLISTS HILL VICTORIAN TOWN**
Ironbridge, UK

The exhibition can only be introduced once all the main building work has been completed. This helps to avoid damage or accidents from scaffolding, moving equipment or other hazards. There need to be clear routes to fire exits, and all materials and constructions must be checked by fire officers. Similarly, the construction of the exhibition must be structurally sound and the safety of the public considered as paramount at all times. At Blists Hill, an eight-projector show was eventually installed in the bays to the right of this image.

Putting on a show   Building an exhibition

Heritage conservation

When making exhibitions in historic buildings or on sensitive archaeological sites the designer needs to be aware of existing conservation rules and regulations, designed to protect the fabric of the existing site. One of the most significant artefacts on display may be the building itself. There will be strict guidelines about attaching exhibition structure to walls and floors, and there may also be conservation implications in terms of heating, humidity and light. It is not unusual to have to design free-standing exhibitions that do not connect in any way with the building. On occasion there are conflicting access and conservation issues that create orientation and interpretation challenges for the exhibition designer.

: DINAH CASSON
Designers are concerned with space, materiality and light. There is a lot of crossover between exhibition and museum design and regular interiors: how people learn and how people engage.

Construction

The majority of exhibitions are constructed from softwood carcasses, to which a 'surface' is applied. This carcass may be plasterboard, flexible medium-density fibreboard (MDF), plywood or a graphic substrate such as Foamex, all finished as specified. Larger exhibition designs may require input from a structural engineer to ensure they are sound. The carcass forms the main body of the exhibition onto which exhibition paraphernalia can be attached.

It is common for the main construction to take place in sections in the contractor's workshop. Care needs to be taken to ensure that prefabricated elements will fit through site access points at the exhibition venue, once they are completed and transported back to the site for erection and finishing.

The complexity and choice of materials for example curved walls and extra levels, will impact on the construction costs and may have access implications. As most flat materials come in standard sizes, consideration of this early in the design process will reduce expense and waste caused by specifications which are just over or under these sizes.

Exhibitions under construction are not only potentially dangerous, but are also dirty and dusty. Like theatrical sets, areas that are not visible to the public are roughly finished, to save time and money. It is only when all building work and finishing is completed that the exhibition environment is left to 'settle'. Dust must be at a minimum before valuable artefacts or products can be displayed or case interiors dressed.

For commercial exhibitions, the exhibitors' manual will give detailed information on maximum heights of stands, public access and etiquette in relation to adjoining exhibition stands. 'Drops' or suspensions points enable structures, banners and lighting rigs to be hung from the ceiling of the hall. Most exhibition halls have a solid concrete floor, with service channels at regular intervals. A 100mm (4in) softwood plinth enables water pipes or electrical cabling to be brought up from the floor, although occasionally electricity is brought in from overhead. Floor coverings are usually the first component of the stand to be put in place, and are covered and secured with a thick plastic sheet for protection. The stand can then be built on top and, once painting is complete, the plastic can be removed. Construction needs to be particularly efficient as a delay in completion often brings with it financial penalties.

= **SITE CONSTRUCTION FOR
A TRADE EXHIBITION,
NATIONAL EXHIBITION CENTRE
Birmingham, UK**

This image shows general construction of a typical exhibition trade show. These booths are being painted and finished before being 'dressed' on site with objects and graphics.

? **FLAT-PACK**
The majority of exhibits are built from flat sheets of materials. Draw a sketch of a simple robot on to a sheet of paper and then try to work out how you could build your simple robot from a single sheet of card taken from the back of a cereal packet.

Putting on a show   Exhibition lighting

= **GREAT NORTH MUSEUM**
  Newcastle upon Tyne, UK

DESIGNER
= **CASSON MANN**

DATE
= **2009**

This image shows a state-of-the-art interpretive treatment
for the Great North Museum's delicate taxidermy collection.
A striking construction of display cases and lightboxes suggests
a layering of the living world; from birds flying above, a selection
of land animals in the central spaces and finally the creatures
of the sea below. An imaginative use of lighting and projection
techniques adds colour and atmosphere to the finished story.

Lighting design is a fascinating but complex discipline and for large exhibition projects the expertise of lighting specialists is invaluable. However, it is important for the exhibition designer to understand the basics of working with light. The aesthetic and narrative opportunities created by light also bring practical implications.

Lighting basics

Lighting involves the use of both natural daylight and artificial light sources (see page 92). In most situations, the exhibition designer will need to work with both. The principal objective for the exhibition designer is to ensure optimum conditions for viewing an object or display. This does not only involve lighting the exhibits themselves but also involves ensuring comfortable visual conditions for the visitor, enabling easy movement and adaptation between displays.

The measure of light perceived by the human eye is measured in lumen or lux (the difference being that lux takes into account the area over which the light is spread). In the US, this is measured in footcandles. The illuminance of daylight (or lux value) is far greater than that of artificial light and this has important implications for museums in particular.

Radiant flux, the measurement of power of light emitted from a source, is measured in watts.

?
SPECIALIST CONTRACTORS
Every specialist contractor working on an exhibition project will require a specific tendering package. Visit your local museum and think about the range of contractors you would need to generate the exhibitions. What information might have been included in their tendering packages?

Putting on a show   Exhibition lighting

Conservation

If given the choice, most exhibition designers would prefer to work in a black box, where they can have complete control over lighting. The reality, however, particularly when designing exhibitions in older buildings, is a compromise between natural daylight and artificial light. Natural light will always be controlled to give the correct level of ambient light, whilst clever, artificial lighting schemes are used for the exhibits.

Light is made up of a spectrum of wavelengths. Both natural and artificial light contain infrared radiation which generates heat. This is potentially harmful to delicate objects and needs to be kept to a minimum. Ultraviolet light (UV), which sits at the opposite end of the light spectrum, can cause natural dyes to fade and plastics to become brittle.

To protect light-sensitive objects from daylight, windows can be obscured, and UV film filters go some way to cutting down exposure. Artificial light is easier to control, as UV levels are lower and many new forms of halogen or LEDs generate very little heat. Vulnerable objects require environments with low lux levels. For example, in displays of historic books and paper, light levels should not exceed 50 lux, whilst for oil paintings, which are more stable, 200 lux will usually suffice. Non-organic objects such as stone are more robust and can be displayed in ambient daylight. It should be remembered that the length of exposure is also important. An object receiving 100 lux in a day can be exposed for two days at 50 lux.

The use of glass cases in museums requires careful management of lighting to avoid glare and multiple reflections, which are particularly troublesome for partially sighted visitors.

Managing light

Initial site surveys help the designer to understand existing lighting conditions on site. This survey will inform the installation of power sockets, control gear and electrical devices during construction and installation. Decisions need to be made early in the design process and should inform the technical communication circulated to the main building contractor.

Lighting designers will sketch up a lighting plan, illustrating the types of luminaire (light fitting) and lamps (bulbs) to be used, and on occasion will generate a storyboard to show lighting changes. Different types of lighting are used for different purposes and several luminaires may be used in one environment.

Quantitative lighting is the amount of light needed for a particular activity. In exhibitions this will be service and safety lighting required for cleaning and safely servicing the environment. It also includes the light required to read graphic panels and signage. In trade shows this will be full voltage tungsten floodlights hanging from the roof.

A quantitative approach considers how light changes the audience perception of a space, changing its mood and atmosphere. Most lighting schemes will use a combination of 'ambient light', which describes the general illumination, 'accent lighting', which dramatically lights one element to create highlights, and 'sparkle' which involves special lighting effects to create a spectacle.

These three types of lighting, used together, build up layers of light and colour. Trade exhibitors often use brightly lit stands to compete with their neighbours. This generates so much heat, that exhibition halls sometimes need ventilation.

Storyboard

A series of captioned visuals explaining a sequence of events, images or views in an audio-visual presentation, exhibition or staged event.

Putting on a show   Exhibition lighting

= **AFRICA PAVILION**
Zaragoza Expo, Spain

DESIGNER
= **ATELIER BRÜCKNER**

DATE
= **2008**

During the day the canopy protects visitors from the sun. The wide walkways in front of the pavilions host music and events, whilst their interiors take advantage of a 'black box' to exploit lighting effects. The Africa pavilion on the left designed by Atelier Brückner shimmers in the sunlight, as the façade is activated by wind and visitor movement. At night its surfaces become an opportunity for light projection, telling the story of weather phenomena in Africa.

Putting on a show Handover

As with any design project, handover to the client can be one of the most difficult and nerve-wracking stages. However, the exhibition designer must remain involved to ensure that the exhibition can be managed and maintained correctly and efficiently.

Snagging

'Snagging' is a collaborative process between the project manager, designer and contractors, carried out to ensure that the exhibition is of an acceptable quality before it is handed over to the client. Snagging lists (also called the 'punch list' in some countries) are lists of problems or defects in the construction or function of the exhibition that come to light at the end of a project. Snagging may include indicative photographs and will include all aspects of the exhibition. Once all the problems have been resolved, the project can be 'signed off' by the client, and final payment can be completed. Once they are finished, museums often open exhibitions 'unofficially' for a test period, in order to help identify problems that can be corrected before the full opening.

= **FOSSIL WALL MODEL,**
THE DEEP
Hull, UK

DESIGNER
= **CSAKY ASSOCIATES**

DATE
= **2002**

For this project, a 'fossil wall' telling the story of the development of life from the sea, was erected over two floors of an aquarium building. This was a complicated environment, involving interactives, sound, light, film and graphics, so clear instructions on how the work was to be carried out safely were crucial. Here we see a model indicating how the wall will be built, the wall in construction and the final design, transformed by lighting.

Handing over an exhibition

When handing over an exhibition to the client, it is one of the design team's final responsibilities to provide a package of information giving clear instructions on how it is to be managed and maintained. This may include everything from instructions on how to get into an exhibit to change a light bulb, to contact details for replenishing the consumables for simple interactives. There should be clear instructions on how to manage multimedia equipment, including contact details of suppliers. It is increasingly more common for permanent galleries to take out maintenance contracts that cover most of these areas.

Putting on a show   Evaluation

Once installed, the design process continues through a process of evaluation and review. Here, valuable lessons can be learned and fed back into future projects.

Reflection

The demanding and fast-paced nature of the design industry makes it tempting to move swiftly between projects without taking the time to critically reflect on completed projects. However, analysis of what elements worked and what was less successful can provide invaluable insight when dealing with future projects. This analysis should not only include design, but should consider systems, sustainability, cost, efficiency and teamwork, providing the opportunity of continuous professional development and the positive underpinning of reputation.

Archiving

By the time a project is finished it usua brings with it a huge sigh of relief and a universal desire to move swiftly onto th next project. However, this is the point when there needs to be a digital and a 'spring clean'. Important documentati needs to be saved to disc, clearly labe and stored. Back-up files may be save in a fireproof separate location. There commercial archives available whose services guarantee to maintain inform in an accessible form and some are available online. Decisions need to be made about what should be kept, and rest should be recycled. Research bc and materials soon become a valuab library resource. A visual record shou be made of the project and added to company and individual portfolios. T creates an ever-growing archive that comes to both represent a company act as a resource for future projects. Finally, good projects should be ente for competitions. This is not only go the design team, and the company, also for the positive evolution of the exhibitions industry.

= **THE LONDON TRANSPORT MUSEUM**
London, UK

DESIGNER
= **RALPH APPELBAUM ASSOCIATES**

DATE
= **2007**

Photograph © Peter Mauss / Esto

'World City Walk' is an installation that forms the dramatic entrance to the refurbished London Transport Museum. Starting from the premise that transport is central to the life of the modern city, there are clusters of 90 monitors showing travel in six cities: London, Tokyo, Paris, New York, New Delhi and Shanghai. The exhibit was created using social networking sites to develop a global network of film-makers and collect their work. Shortlisted films were used in the installation. The project continues to evolve and is an impressive example of how an exhibit can extend out from itself, in this case generating an evolving transport archive of its own.

Putting on a show Student case study

PROJECT
= **VISITOR CENTRE FOR THE 2012 OLYMPIC GAMES IN LONDON**

DESIGNER
= **LAURA PARKER**

DATE
= **2010**

! This imagined student brief was to design a Visitor Centre in Hyde Park in London for the 2012 Olympic Games. The exhibition is central to a series of much smaller 'hubs' placed around the city in the run-up to the games. Temporary in structure, the building will house an exhibition that aims to be entertaining, exciting, educational and informative and is aimed at an international audience. Visitors will learn about the games, their impact on the city, breaking news about developments, and will also be able to buy tickets for the games.

For this design concept, the fragmented logo was an inspiration for many of the 3D exhibition features and other important iconic Olympic imagery was also used. The client presentation plan showed the materials to be used as well as sectional elevations and computer-rendered elevations of what the space might look like.

? Imagine you have been asked to design a small, 'black box' pavilion at an expo. Measuring 6x6x6m (20x20x20ft), the theme of the pavilion is 'Space Tourism: Your Journey into Space'. You have been asked to design a simple interactive space that delivers a visitor experience inspired by this theme.

1 Sort out your storyline using mind maps and bubble diagrams as your guide. Who is your audience?

2 Decide on the spatial arrangements by exploring 2D sketching and 3D sketch modelling. Once you have decided on a proposal, make a white card scale model and generate a series of A2 boards expressing your process and a range of ideas, to include hand- or computer-generated visuals.

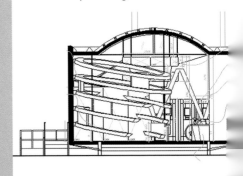

3 Draw a client presentation plan illustrating the key elements of your design and the orientation of visitors passing through your space.

= This sectional elevation forms part of a suite of drawings that would enable a contractor and exhibition specialists to build the scheme.

4 Draw general arrangement orthographics showing a plan, two elevations and a section of your scheme, using the correct orthographic conventions.

Floor covering

Floor covering

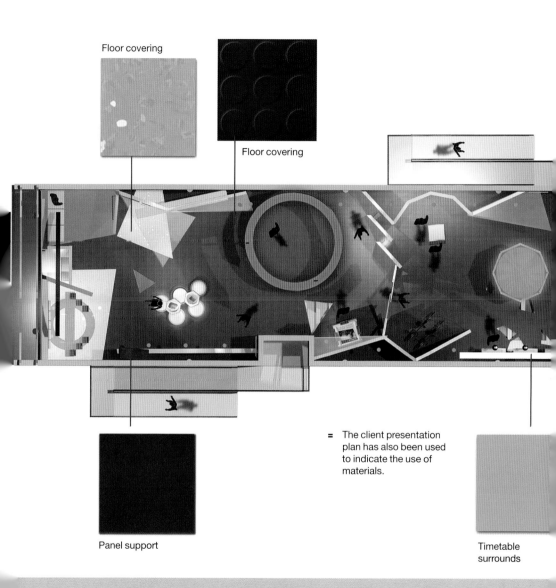

= The client presentation
plan has also been used
to indicate the use of
materials.

Panel support

Timetable
surrounds

= Computer-rendered
visuals indicate how the
exhibition might 'look'.

Conclusion

The very nature of exhibitions means that each is a unique event. Every exhibition tells stories that can be interpreted in many different ways, providing layer upon layer of creative opportunity. This book has been loosely laid out to follow the threads of the design process, so as to help you to navigate a logical path towards designing exhibitions. Hopefully you have been challenged by the thinking points and this conclusion aims to be the final one.

The process of exhibition design is predominantly about conversations. When in search of the 'big idea', there will be a series of personal conversations that take place between hand and head. Digital or analogue, drawing operates by constantly discussing ideas and possibilities with the imagination. Round and round the conversation will go. Sketching and rejecting, questioning and compromising, modelling and making, serendipitous or obvious, the designer will tease out the ideas seen in the mind's eye, nervously developing them to a point when the proposal can be shared.

The client presentation is a very public conversation, when the project proposal has to be presented and sometimes fought for, justified and delivered. Success will introduce a series of technical conversations using a very particular design dialect that is universally understood by makers. Technical drawings finally test the 'buildability' of a design idea. What is it made from? How is it constructed? Is it safe? Is it sustainable? Is it accessible? Does it work? Is it beautiful? Is it what the client wants? Is it what is really needed? Discussions move on from the drawing board, to the workstation, to the workshop and to the world.

And so, eventually, comes the installation of the exhibition. This is the final statement. There is a short pause to gather thoughts, before the personal conversations restart. What worked well? What did not? Evaluate, archive and think about how this informs the next project.

Whilst it is hoped that there are many broad principles in this book that students of design will find useful, there are no 'magic recipes' for designing exhibitions. The joy and variety of different approaches, which have evolved with each generation of designers, is testament to this.

The provision of a toolbox of techniques is meant to be a useful prompt for beginners. However, it should be remembered that there is a great blurring of boundaries between these ideas, and successful design is an illustration of exhibition techniques working harmoniously together. Theatrical, cinematic, interactive, display and graphic visuals; what combination of exhibition techniques will be used? This should always depend upon the nature of the audience. Elegant white plinths, supporting precious objects that are dramatically lit, may subliminally communicate 'do not touch'. But this is no less a theatrical presentation of the 'power of display' than the bold expo pavilions that put on their party best, and show off new and clever toys and technologies to the world!

The messages delivered by an exhibition are driven by the client; the method of delivery is championed by the designer. This may be a quiet whisper or the noisy fun of the fair.

In these days of virtual technologies, the cultural exhibition gives us a valuable and tangible connection to the past. Human beings enjoy seeing 'real' objects, such as historical celebrities, as the blockbuster exhibitions of recent years have shown.

Exhibitions give us the pleasure of 'differentness', they take us away from the ordinary and place us in specially constructed, communicative environments. We may hear conversations from the past through historic collections, or we may seek out the promise of the future through the persuasive marketing of a brand.

However these stories are acted out, it will be the exhibition designer who has the challenge and satisfaction of designing the set.

Useful resources

Bibliography

Allwood, J. Revisited by Ted Allen
and Patrick Reid. 'The Great Exhibitions'
Studio Vista, *London. 2001*

Alphonso, F. Expo Movement, Universal
exhibitions and Spain's contribution *Espana
Expone, Spain. 2008*

Bertron Schwarz Frey Designing Exhibitions
Birkhäuser, Germany. 2006

Best, K. Design Management. Managing
Design Strategy, Process and Implementation
AVA Academia, Switzerland. 2006

Black, M. Exhibition Design
Architectural Press, London. 1950

Carter (Ed), DeMao and Wheeler
'Working with Type – Exhibitions'
Rotovision, Switzerland. 2000

Dean, D. Museum Exhibition
Routledge, London. 1994

Dernie, D. Exhibition Design
Laurence King Publishing Ltd. 2006

Dreyfuss, H. Designing for People
Simon and Schuster, New York. 1955

Gardner, J and Heller, C. 'Exhibition
and Display' *Batsford London. 1960*

Garn, A. Exit to Tomorrow; World's Fair
Architecture, Design, Fashion 1933–2005.
Universe Publishing, New York. 2007

Hall, M. 'On Display' A Design Grammar
for Museum Exhibitions *Lund Humphries,
London. 1987*

Hooper-Greenhill, E. Museum, Media,
Message *Routledge, New York. 1995*

Hooper-Greenhill, E. The Educational
Role of the Museum *Routledge,
New York. 1999*

Hughes, P. Exhibition Design
Laurence King Publishing Ltd, London. 2010

Jackson, A. Expo International Expositions
1851–2010 *V&A Publishing, London. 2008*

Kemp, M Leonardo Da Vinci; Experience,
Experiment, *Design 2007*

Kirkham, P. Charles and Ray Eames
Designers of the Twentieth Century
MIT Press Cambridge, Massachusetts. 1995

Lichtenstein, C & Habärli W (Editors)
Bruno Munari Air Made Visible.
Lars Muller Publishers, Zürich. 2000

Lorenc J/Skolnick, L/ Berger, C.
What is Exhibition Design? *Rotovision SA. 2007*

MacLeod, S. (Ed). Reshaping Museum Space.
Architecture, design, exhibitions. *Routledge,
New York. 2005*

Mattie, E. World's Fairs *Princeton
Architectural Press, New York. 1998*

Perfect, C. and Austen, J.
The Complete Typographer *Rockport
Publishers, Massachusetts. 1992*

Staniszewski. M. The Power of Display:
A History of Exhibition Installations at the
Museum of Modern Art. *MIT Press.
Cambridge, MA. 1998*

Tildon, F. Interpreting Our Heritage.
*Third Edition. Chapel Hill, USA University
of North Carolina Press. 1977*

Velarde, G. Designing Exhibitions.
Museums, Heritage, Trade and World Fairs
*(Second Edition) Ashgate Publishing Ltd,
Aldershot. 2001*

Organisations

Erco
www.erco.com

Event Supplier and Services
Association (ESSA)
www.aeo.org.uk

Expomuseum
www.expomuseum.com

National Trust (UK)
www.nationaltrust.org.uk

National Trust for Historic Preservation (US)
www.preservationnation.org

UNESCO World Heritage Sites
www.unesco.org

United Nations Global Compact
www.unglobalcompact.org

Designers and exhibition companies

Atelier Brückner
www.atelier-bruckner.de

At Large
www.atlarge.co.uk

ATS Heritage
www.ats-heritage.co.uk

Bremner and Orr
www.bremnerandorr.com

Casson Mann
www.cassonmann.co.uk

Checkland Kindleysides
www.checklandkindleysides.com

Cultural Innovations
www.culturalinnovations.com

Diller, Scofidio + Renfro
www.dsrny.com

Event Communications
www.eventcomm.com

Furneaux Stewart Design
www.furneauxstewart.com

Gewerk Design
www.gewerk.com

Imagination
www.imagination.com

Land Design Studio
www.landdesignstudio.co.uk

Mauk Design
www.maukdesign.com

Metaphor
www.mphor.co.uk

Neal Potter Design Associates
www.nealpotterdesign.co.uk

Nick Bell Design
www.nickbelldesign.co.uk

Photosound
www.photosound.co.uk

Ralph Appelbaum Associates
www.raany.com

Redman Design
www.redman-design.com

Octonorm
www.octanorm.co.uk

Pentagram
www.pentagram.com

Vertigo Systems GMBH
www.vertigo-systems.de

Museums

Guggenheim, Bilbao, Spain
www.guggenheim.org

Museum of Modern Art, New York, US
www.moma.org

National Cold War Museum, Cosford, UK
www.nationalcoldwarexhibition.org

Natural History Museum, London, UK
www.nhm.ac.uk

Pitt Rivers Museum, Oxford, UK
www.prm.ox.ac.uk

Quai Branly, Paris, France
www.quaibranly.fr

Smithsonian, Washington DC, US
www.si.edu

Sovereign Hill, Ballarat, Australia
www.sovereignhill.com/au

The Getty, Los Angeles, US
www.getty.edu

The Museum of Communication, Bern,
Switzerland
www.mfk.ch

Victoria and Albert Museum, London, UK
www.vam.ac.uk

Glossary

Accessibility

Many countries now require by law public buildings to be planned in accordance with a regulatory framework that enables accessibility for all visitors. This might take the form of minimum doorway widths, handrail heights, gradients of ramps and provision of materials for deaf or blind visitors.

Anthropometrics

The comparative study of the sizes and proportions of the human body. A knowledge of anthropometric proportions enables the designer to create spaces that are comfortable, efficient and enjoyable to use.

Audience

The people who attend an exhibition. Exhibition designers will often design with a specific audience in mind but it is important to try to keep the design open to as wide an audience as possible.

Axonometric

Scaled drawing achieved by projecting in the vertical axis directly from the plan (often drawn at 45°).

Bespoke

Specifically designed or 'tailor made'.

Brand

A brand can be a person, a product or a logo. Anything that can be bought or sold as an idea or artefact can be a brand.

Briefing process

A dialogue between client and designer, which produces a progressively more adequate or detailed design brief.

Chronological order

A record of events based on the order in which they occurred.

Colour swatches

Samples of a material in a range of colours. These enable the designer to make judgements about how final finishes might look in a design scheme.

Conservation

The preservation, restoration or renovation of something. Exhibitions require a sound knowledge and awareness of conservation issues and the impact that they have on the design process.

Contract

A legally binding agreement between two or more people or parties, usually specified in a document detailing the terms and conditions of an exchange of services and/ or goods for remuneration or reward.

Contractor

In the exhibition context, the main contractor undertakes to produce and install the main structure of an exhibition. Specialist contractors offer goods or services relating to the delivery of an exhibition.

Design process

An ideal or generic model of design activity from start to finish.

Design proposal

A coherent solution to the problem(s) set out in the project brief. Usually presented to a client through a professional presentation which may include, perspective visuals, plans and elevations, 3D models, graphic visuals, storyboards and a design report.

Detailed drawing

A working drawing showing a high level of detail. Usually drawn in section full size or 1:5 and cross-referenced to a general arrangement drawing. Normally orthographic, sometimes isometric or axonometric projection.

Development sketch(es)

One of a series of drawings, normally freehand, showing a progression of design ideas through concept and detailed design phases.

Elevation

A drawing projected from the horizontal axis. In the context of interiors, normally a sectional elevation showing the walls, floor and ceiling in section and the size and position of all exhibits and other significant features in elevation. In free-standing exhibits, exterior elevations are normally shown first.

Evaluation

The results are used to improve the quality of the final product or the process of designing and producing it.

Exhibit

Any organised combination of objects, information in graphic, typographic and audio-visual form, supporting structure, and enclosure or housing, which is designed to communicate. A single module within an exhibition.

Exhibition

Any organised assemblage of exhibits which is designed to serve an overall purpose or present a theme or narrative.

Expo

A large international exhibition.

General Arrangement (GA) drawing

An orthographic drawing dimensioned to show size and position of all significant elements, and annotated to identify each element and specify materials, methods of construction and finishes. All subsequent working drawings and detailed drawings are cross-referenced to the GA drawing. Normally an exhibition includes a GA plan showing the exhibit / exhibition site location.

Graphic layout

A dimensional and annotated scale drawing of a graphic design showing size and position of all significant graphic elements. Generated digitally.

Graphics

A combination of words and images designed to convey a message.

Installation

A site-specific form of art. Installations will always have a direct relationship with their surroundings and will be interpreted as such.

Interactivity

An activity involving a two-way flow of information between a device and a user.

Interpretive scheme

The information structure or narrative framework used to guide the development of storylines.

Isometric drawing

A drawing to scale such that each perpendicular axis is shown at 120 degrees to the others.

Glossary

Material boards

Samples of materials to give an impression of the texture, appearance and durability of a material. These are useful when considering the finishes to a design scheme.

Orientation

Wayfinding, informing visitors, by way of signposts, maps, and trails, where they are, and where they are going.

Orthographic drawing

Measured scale drawing showing plan (or plan section) and elevations (or sectional elevations) on the same sheet. Views are taken at right angles to each other and presented in a conventional format.

Plan

A drawing projected from the vertical axis, looking down (inverted plan looking up). In the exhibition context, normally a plan section drawing showing the layout of exhibits and other significant elements as if sliced through at eye level to reveal doorways, windows and the interiors of displays.

Presentation

The design proposal as communicated to the client. Also the act of communicating a design proposal.

Presentation model

3D model in colour or in white showing content and construction. This may be produced digitally and include an animated walkthrough.

Presentation visual

Coloured perspective representation of the designed object indicating what the object will 'look like'.

Proportion

The relationship between the parts and dimensions of an element. Common proportion systems used in design include the Fibonacci sequence and the golden section.

Proposal

A plan put forward for the consideration of a client. The exhibition designer will put together a proposal containing sketches, plans, detailed drawings and models of their design ideas. Feedback from the client will be used to further develop and fine-tune the design proposal.

Rendering

In the design context, the act of applying accurate shading and colour to a drawing - usually applied to constructed drawings.

Scale

A measuring system based on the size of something in relation to something else. Design drawings are usually drawn on a small scale though details are sometimes drawn at full scale.

Section

A drawing in which the object is imagined to be cut through in a particular plane hence plan section and sectional elevation.

Site

The location in which a design is to be implemented. This might take the form of an existing building, a piece of land or a specially-created space.

Sketch

A rough drawing, often used to create more detailed drawings or to promote new ideas.

Sketch model

Preliminary 3D model intended to suggest spatial layout, form and/or content. Often used in personal design conversations using recyclable materials.

Specifications

Details of dimensions, materials, methods of production, finishes, etc. required to produce and install an exhibit or exhibition. In complex work they are also normally produced as a written document (see: Tendering package).

Storyboard

A series of captioned visuals explaining a sequence of events, images or views in an audio-visual presentation, exhibition or staged event.

Storyline

A written description of the narrative content of an exhibition or event.

Sustainability

The sensible use of natural resources in design and building work to ensure that valuable resources are not depleted or wasted. Sustainability is of increasing importance to designers across the world.

Tendering package

A combination of documents and drawings offered to potential contractors for the purpose of estimating costs or quoting a price. Normally includes: a letter inviting to tender, general arrangement drawing, working drawings, detailed written specifications (including general clauses and conditions).

Typography

The design of letterforms and their combination and arrangement to communicate a message to the desired effect.

Working drawing

Orthographic drawing explaining construction and assembly to those involved in the manufacture of the work. Includes: detailed dimensions, and specification of materials, methods of construction, finishes, fixings and fittings. Normally cross-referenced to a general arrangement drawing.

X-height

Height of the lower-case 'x' in a designed typeface – varies from typeface to typeface. The 'x' height (with no ascender or descender) represents the 'mass' or 'body' of the typeface.

Index

Page numbers in italics refer to illustrations

Acknowledgements

My thanks go out to friends and colleagues from the University of Lincoln for their help in writing this book. These include Len Rye, Chris Hay, Doug Gittens, Karen Bartlett and Dave Bramston and in particular Dr Jane Lomholt, Dr Geoff Matthews and Dick McConnell for their practical help, personal support and encyclopaedic knowledge.

Many thanks to the students and graduates of BA (Hons) Design for Exhibition & Museums, who supplied their exemplary work. My special thanks go to Hwee Li Ng, Lisa Martin, Hans Chua, Lindsay Barchan, Geoff Bellingham, Agnes Tan, Ailsa Early, Rachel Otterway, Sarah Matthews, Jon Helly Clements and Peter MacDermid for their help with illustrations and images.

Thank you to all our friends from the exhibition and museum industry, who continue to support design education and who have generously contributed to this book. Thank you to Catherine Armour for her comments early on in the process. Also special thanks to Leafy Robinson at AVA for her support and kindness during challenging times.

Thank you to, Jennifer, Emily and Phillip Locker, for their enthusiasm, good humour and support and most importantly of all, to Dr Ian Locker for his endless encouragement and love.

Index compiled by Indexing Specialists (UK) Ltd, Indexing House, 306A Portland Road, Hove, East Sussex BN3 6LP. Tel: 01273 416777. email: indexers@indexing.co.uk www.indexing.co.uk

BASICS
INTERIOR DESIGN

Lynne Elvins
Naomi Goulder

Working with ethics

Publisher's note

The subject of ethics is not new, yet its consideration within the applied visual arts is perhaps not as prevalent as it might be. Our aim here is to help a new generation of students, educators and practitioners find a methodology for structuring their thoughts and reflections in this vital area.

AVA Publishing hopes that these **Working with ethics** pages provide a platform for consideration and a flexible method for incorporating ethical concerns in the work of educators, students and professionals. Our approach consists of four parts:

The **introduction** is intended to be an accessible snapshot of the ethical landscape, both in terms of historical development and current dominant themes.

The **framework** positions ethical consideration into four areas and poses questions about the practical implications that might occur. Marking your response to each of these questions on the scale shown will allow your reactions to be further explored by comparison.

The **case study** sets out a real project and then poses some ethical questions for further consideration. This is a focus point for a debate rather than a critical analysis so there are no predetermined right or wrong answers.

A selection of **further reading** for you to consider areas of particular interest in more detail.

aware-
ness/
reflect-
ion/
debate

Introduction

Ethics is a complex subject that interlaces the idea of responsibilities to society with a wide range of considerations relevant to the character and happiness of the individual. It concerns virtues of compassion, loyalty and strength, but also of confidence, imagination, humour and optimism. As introduced in ancient Greek philosophy, the fundamental ethical question is: *what should I do?* How we might pursue a 'good' life not only raises moral concerns about the effects of our actions on others, but also personal concerns about our own integrity.

In modern times the most important and controversial questions in ethics have been the moral ones. With growing populations and improvements in mobility and communications, it is not surprising that considerations about how to structure our lives together on the planet should come to the forefront. For visual artists and communicators, it should be no surprise that these considerations will enter into the creative process.

Some ethical considerations are already enshrined in government laws and regulations or in professional codes of conduct. For example, plagiarism and breaches of confidentiality can be punishable offences. Legislation in various nations makes it unlawful to exclude people with disabilities from accessing information or spaces. The trade of ivory as a material has been banned in many countries. In these cases, a clear line has been drawn under what is unacceptable.

But most ethical matters remain open to debate, among experts and lay-people alike, and in the end we have to make our own choices on the basis of our own guiding principles or values. Is it more ethical to work for a charity than for a commercial company? Is it unethical to create something that others find ugly or offensive?

Specific questions such as these may lead to other questions that are more abstract. For example, is it only effects on humans (and what they care about) that are important, or might effects on the natural world require attention too?

Is promoting ethical consequences justified even when it requires ethical sacrifices along the way? Must there be a single unifying theory of ethics (such as the Utilitarian thesis that the right course of action is always the one that leads to the greatest happiness of the greatest number), or might there always be many different ethical values that pull a person in various directions?

As we enter into ethical debate and engage with these dilemmas on a personal and professional level, we may change our views or change our view of others. The real test though is whether, as we reflect on these matters, we change the way we act as well as the way we think. Socrates, the 'father' of philosophy, proposed that people will naturally do 'good' if they know what is right. But this point might only lead us to yet another question: *how do we know what is right?*

YOU

What are your ethical beliefs?

Central to everything you do will be your attitude to people and issues around you. For some people, their ethics are an active part of the decisions they make every day as a consumer, a voter or a working professional. Others may think about ethics very little and yet this does not automatically make them unethical. Personal beliefs, lifestyle, politics, nationality, religion, gender, class or education can all influence your ethical viewpoint.

Using the scale, where would you place yourself? What do you take into account to make your decision? Compare results with your friends or colleagues.

YOUR CLIENT

What are your terms?

Working relationships are central to whether ethics can be embedded into a project, and your conduct on a day-to-day basis is a demonstration of your professional ethics. The decision with the biggest impact is whom you choose to work with in the first place. Cigarette companies or arms traders are often-cited examples when talking about where a line might be drawn, but rarely are real situations so extreme. At what point might you turn down a project on ethical grounds and how much does the reality of having to earn a living affect your ability to choose?

Using the scale, where would you place a project? How does this compare to your personal ethical level?

01 02 03 04 05 06 07 08 09 10

01 02 03 04 05 06 07 08 09 10

YOUR SPECIFICATIONS

What are the impacts of your materials?

In relatively recent times, we are learning that many natural materials are in short supply. At the same time, we are increasingly aware that some man-made materials can have harmful, long-term effects on people or the planet. How much do you know about the materials that you use? Do you know where they come from, how far they travel and under what conditions they are obtained? When your creation is no longer needed, will it be easy and safe to recycle? Will it disappear without a trace? Are these considerations your responsibility or are they out of your hands?

Using the scale, mark how ethical your material choices are.

YOUR CREATION

What is the purpose of your work?

Between you, your colleagues and an agreed brief, what will your creation achieve? What purpose will it have in society and will it make a positive contribution? Should your work result in more than commercial success or industry awards? Might your creation help save lives, educate, protect or inspire? Form and function are two established aspects of judging a creation, but there is little consensus on the obligations of visual artists and communicators toward society, or the role they might have in solving social or environmental problems. If you want recognition for being the creator, how responsible are you for what you create and where might that responsibility end?

Using the scale, mark how ethical the purpose of your work is.

01 02 03 04 05 06 07 08 09 10

01 02 03 04 05 06 07 08 09 10

The Shakers

One aspect of interior design that raises an ethical dilemma is that of creating interior spaces that may directly affect people's health and well-being. For example, some studies have found concentrations of VOCs (volatile organic compounds) up to ten times higher indoors than outdoors. VOCs are emitted, amongst other things, by paints, lacquers, flooring materials and furnishings.
The adverse health effects of over exposure to harmful VOCs can include eye and throat irritation, headaches, fatigue, dizziness and nausea. Electrical fields generated by everyday equipment, such as computers, and excess static electricity created by certain materials, could also be bad for human health. Prolonged exposure to electrical fields may cause increased risk of respiratory diseases and infection, airborne bacteria and viruses. At what point should (or do) interior design projects take into account these and other health issues? Is it the responsibility of the interior designer to consider potential risks based on inconclusive evidence that is still being explored and debated? Or is it the responsibility of scientific researchers and governments working with the manufacturers of the materials under question?

The Shakers were a religious sect that went to America from England in 1774 seeking freedom from religious persecution. They pursued complete independence from 'the outside world', which led them to build their own properties and design their own objects.

Shaker interiors were entirely free of ornament, contrasting starkly with the mainstream excesses of the Victorian appetite for the fancy and elaborate. Beadings or mouldings were stripped away. Walls were plain white and painted floors were kept bare for easy cleaning. On entering a Shaker building, one commentator wrote: 'The first impression of all is cleanliness with a suggestion of bareness which is not inconsistent, however, with comfort, and which comes chiefly from the aspect of unpapered walls, the scrubbed floors hidden only by rugs and strips of carpeting, and the plain flat finish of the woodwork.'

Window frames, chimneys and stairways were all executed with clean lines in basic forms. The results reflected total simplicity, remarkable functionality and beautifully proportioned craftsmanship. Shakers designed everything with careful thought, working with the belief that to produce something well was in itself 'an act of prayer'.

Shakers lived communal lives, so furniture was built and arranged for efficient use by large numbers of people. Everything was functional, including chairs, benches, tables and huge banks of storage cabinets with drawers. Lines of wooden pegs around a room were used to hang up chairs, baskets and hats. Furniture was made out of pine or other inexpensive wood, and so was light in colour and weight. The interior of Shaker meeting houses included large, open floor space to allow for their religious dances. The important factors within any building were considered to be the quality of light, an equal distribution of heat, general care for protection and comfort, and other factors that pertained to health and long life. Typical communal bedrooms might contain simple rope beds, washbasins and wood-burning stoves. Storage boxes, clocks, brooms and woven materials were also created, with some products made available to sell.

By the middle of the twentieth century, collectors, inspired by the modernist assertion that 'form follows function', were drawn to Shaker artefacts at the same time as Shaker communities were themselves disappearing. Original Shaker furniture is costly and still sought after today, due to its quality and historical significance.

If an interior design is inspired by religious belief, does it make the result more ethical?

How might decoration seem more unethical than plainness?

Would you work on providing a Shaker interior to a wealthy private client?

WILLIAM MORRIS
Ornamental pattern work, to be raised above the contempt of reasonable men, must possess three qualities: beauty, imagination and order.

AIGA
Design Business and Ethics
2007, AIGA

Eaton, Marcia Muelder
Aesthetics and the Good Life
1989, Associated University Press

Ellison, David
Ethics and Aesthetics in European Modernist Literature:
From the Sublime to the Uncanny
2001, Cambridge University Press

Fenner, David E W (Ed)
Ethics and the Arts:
An Anthology
1995, Garland Reference Library of Social Science

Gini, Al and Marcoux, Alexei M
Case Studies in Business Ethics
2005, Prentice Hall

McDonough, William and Braungart, Michael
Cradle to Cradle:
Remaking the Way We Make Things
2002, North Point Press

Papanek, Victor
Design for the Real World:
Making to Measure
1972, Thames & Hudson

United Nations Global Compact
The Ten Principles
www.unglobalcompact.org/AboutTheGC/TheTenPrinciples/index.html